N~~O~~T
A WRITER...
∧I AM J~~U~~ST IN GRADUATE SCHOOL:
AND

A Guide to Writing Critically, Clearly and Coherently

I AM ~~NOT~~ A WRITER...

∧I AM ~~JUST~~ IN GRADUATE SCHOOL:
AND

A Guide to Writing Critically, Clearly and Coherently

Vernetta K. Williams, PhD

The publication of I'm Not a Writer

Copyright © 2016 by Vernetta K. Williams PhD

All rights reserved. No part of this publication may be reproduced or transmitted in any form or by any means, electronic or mechanical, including photocopy, recording, or any information storage and retrieval system, *without* permission in writing from the publisher.

Published by
Chrysalis Consulting LLC
PO Box 82314
Tampa, FL 33682

All rights reserved.

ISBN-13: 978-1533392916
ISBN-10: 1533392919

Cover and Interior design: Tyeroh, Inc.

Dedication

To the faculty members, administrators and mentors who directly ensured that I progressed academically and professionally to earn a PhD in English: Dr. Patricia Bonner, Dr. Judy Genshaft, Dr. Hunt Hawkins, Deborah Love, J.D., Dr. Gary Olson, Dr. Dwayne Smith, Dr. Brenda Walker, Dr. Lynn Worsham and the late Drs. Charles Heglar and Jack Moore.

Acknowledgments

No individual labor of love is completed without meaningful contributions from multiple people. This book project is no exception; I truly enjoy a phenomenal network of colleagues, mentors and advisors who helped me finish this guide.

Thank you Dr. Elizabeth A. Metzger for inviting me years ago, as a newly minted PhD, to co-present graduate writing workshops. You expressed confidence in me when I doubted my ability to utilize my credentials to help doctoral students develop as academic writers.

Thank you Dr. Lawrence Morehouse, the dedicated staff at the Florida Education Fund and McKnight Fellows for welcoming me into your community of scholars and providing a platform for exploring my ideas to meet graduate student writing needs.

Thank you University of South Florida (USF) faculty members Drs. Joe Moxley, Uday Murthy, Kathi Katz and Kevin Sellers for reviewing this guide. Your thoughtful feedback challenged me to revisit vital aspects of the book and strengthen its value, content and academic merit. Also, thank you Dr. Murthy for permission to incorporate your research paper guide into an appendix.

Thank you Dr. Terry Engle for stopping to chat with me in Starbucks; that one conversation led to several insightful dialogues and ideas. Every time I have been in Starbucks to write, your smile and kind words have encouraged me.

Thank you Mr. Gary Oliver, Assistant Director of Graduate Student Services, USF Office of Graduate Studies and Joe Ford, J.D., Assistant VP of USF Health Shared Student Services, for partnering with me to offer graduate writing workshops at USF. You both possess an amazing commitment to servicing the ongoing needs of graduate students.

Thank you Dr. Melanie Michaels for graciously extending the opportunity to present to students in the DNP program in the USF College of Nursing so that I could become intimately acquainted with health-related writing issues as well as evidence-based writing requirements.

Thank you to the numerous graduate students who have trusted me to edit your works, teach you principles of research based writing, coach you in your scholarly writing development and help you navigate sensitive areas of advanced graduate study. Because of you, I continually improve my abilities to instruct, mentor and encourage.

I especially would like to thank the future Drs. Tara Nkrumah and Amanda Albright; your initiative in utilizing all resources to become the best scholars you can is inspiring. You motivate me to share all that I know; it has been an honor to be part of your educational journeys. Thank you so much for allowing me to include examples of your writing in this guide to illustrate concepts presented.

ACKNOWLEDGMENTS

Thank you immensely Dr. Sylvia Holladay for proofreading the book and giving final suggestions; it is wonderful to have a colleague with more knowledge, expertise and experience to perfect my writing. Thank you Anthony Jones of Tyeroh Graphics for bringing my vision of the cover to life.

Introduction

Too many students struggle unnecessarily with their writing at the graduate level. Yes, writing expectations, demands and requirements of master's and doctoral programs are daunting; nevertheless, writing is a skill that can and must be mastered in order to earn a graduate degree.

Higher education culture, referred to as the ivory tower for its wholehearted commitment to intellectual pursuit, is best reflected in those who can articulate their academic acumen through scholarly publication. Graduate study remains the vehicle through which promising scholars demonstrate their proficiency to engage in academic inquiry at the highest level.

I'm Not a Writer...I'm just in Graduate School is a practical resource that acclimates graduate students to scholarly writing by providing valuable strategies, information and examples. The guide's contents are based on the author's writing knowledge and expertise as an English PhD as well as her professional experiences teaching writing courses at the university level, editing scholarly works, presenting writing workshops on college campuses and coaching master's and doctoral level students in scholarly writing development.

The competencies needed to compose scholarship often are not explained fully in graduate school, yet students must develop and demonstrate them. When graduate students do not possess these skills, their educational progress halts and hope of earning an advanced degree vanishes. *I'm Not a Writer...I'm just in Graduate School* delineates the writing techniques and non-writing aspects of graduate study indispensable for effectively producing scholarly writing in an understandable way. The first two chapters explain the unique educational culture of advanced study, including what being a scholar means. Chapters three, four and five provide an in-depth look at the writing process, with examples of actual graduate students' works to illustrate concepts. Chapter six explores the attitude and actions required to produce success at the graduate level. Advice from graduate students is dispersed throughout the guide. The guide ends with four appendices that provide the following practical information: 1) a narrative reflection of the author's journey from student to scholar, 2) a checklist for sections of a research paper, 3) a reference resource list of graduate level writing resources and 4) a list of common transitions.

I'm Not a Writer...I'm just in Graduate School targets those in traditional PhD programs. However, master's students and those in applied/practitioner based advanced degree programs also must mature academically and rhetorically in order to produce scholarship; therefore, they will benefit from reading this guide as well.

CONTENTS

DEDICATION	v
ACKNOWLEDGMENTS	vii
INTRODUCTION	xi

1 Learn the Mysterious Expectations of Graduate School   1

Realize that Writing Issues Are Common	1
Address Writing Issues Early	4
Know Graduate Faculty Writing Expectations	6
Important Writing Skills for Graduate Students to Master	8
Respond to Graduate Faculty Writing Expectations	8
Consider the Writing Center: A Traditional Writing Resource	9
Recognize that Scholarly Writing Is More Than Writing	11
Shed the Undergraduate Mentality About Education and Writing	12
Make a Mental Paradigm Shift	13
Expectations of Graduate Students	15

2 Become a Scholar   17

Learn the Academic Conversation	18
Read Scholarship Critically	20
Advice from Seasoned Graduate Students	22
Develop an Authoritative Scholarly Voice	23
Improve Critical Reading and Critical Thinking	24
Embrace the Scholar's Responsibility to Write	25
Prepare for the Scholarly Rite of Passage	26
Dissertation Advice from Doctoral Candidates	28
Expect to Write Beyond the Degree	29

3 Develop a Systematic Approach to Writing — 31

Understand the Writing Process	31
Stage One: Prewrite	32
Consider Audience	34
Pinpoint a Primary Purpose	36
Compose a Working Thesis	36
Utilize Prewriting Techniques	38
Annotate	39
Brainstorm/List	42
Free write	43
Cluster/Map	45
Question	46
Discuss	47
Outline	48
Example of Outlining to Organize Research and Ideas	49
Journal	52

4 Draft Properly — 55

Stage Two: Draft	55
Master the Body Paragraph	56
Formulate a Topic Sentence	57
Provide Supporting Sentences	57
Add Detailing Sentences	57
Compose a Concluding Sentence	58
Sample Body Paragraph	58
Body Paragraph from a Dissertation	59
Incorporate and Cite Research Properly	61
Graduate Student Advice on Research	64
Write Introduction and Conclusion Paragraphs	65
Remember the Goal of Drafting	66

CONTENTS

5 Understand All Editing Is Not the Same — 69

Stage Three: Revise — 69
Answer Specific Questions When Revising — 70
Improve Coherence — 72
Learn Useful Coherence Devices — 73
Incorporate Transitional Words, Phrases and Sentences — 74
Understand Parallel Constructions — 75
Repeat Key Terms — 77
Create a Reading Rhythm — 78
Stage Four: Proofread — 79
Avoid Blending the Two Types of Editing — 80
Make the Right Assumption — 81
Utilize Proofreading Techniques — 81
Differentiate between Style and Grammar — 82
Access Academic Resources to Master Style — 85
Personalize the Writing Process — 86
Advice from Graduate Students on Writing — 88

6 Take Ownership of Graduate Education — 89

Be Committed — 89
Be Proactive — 90
Be Professional — 92
Traits of a Professional — 93
Advice from Graduate Students on Earning an Advanced Degree — 95
Conclusion — 96

ABOUT THE AUTHOR — 97

APPENDICES   99

- Appendix A: Author Reflections on Her Journey from Student to Scholar   99
- Appendix B: A Guide to Writing a Research Paper, Composed by Dr. Uday S. Murthy, Director, Lynn Pippenger School of Accountancy, Eminent Scholar, University of South Florida Muma College of Business   113
- Appendix C: Reference Resource List for Scholarly Writing Development   119
- Appendix D: A List of Common Transitional Words, Adopted from Purdue University's OWL (Online Writing Lab)   121

WORKS CITED   123

CHAPTER | 1

Learn the Mysterious Expectations of Graduate School

Frustration. Anxiety. Confusion. Isolation. Stress. These emotions typically bombard first year graduate students as they attempt to navigate the daunting new world of advanced academic study. Many master's and doctoral level students quickly become overwhelmed by the intense demands of graduate school, which include heavy reading loads, intense writing assignments and meticulous research requirements that must be completed within a short turnaround time.

Realize that Writing Issues Are Common

Scholarship on graduate student writing confirms that most students enter graduate programs ill-equipped to write at a scholarly level and struggle to produce sound academic arguments (Badenhorst et al. 9; Carter 408; Mullen 119; Ondrusek 185; Sallee, Hallett and Tierney 69). However, graduate students often concentrate on other academic skills, not the development of their writing. In fact, much of the early focus of new graduate students is mastering effective time management since many students struggle to acclimate to the rigorous reading and research demands of graduate school (Nelson, Range and Ross 376; Weisblat and Sell 65). Assignment due dates are constant and often inflexible, so the priority of most students becomes staying current on readings, preparing for class discussions and planning presentations.

The pervasive pressure of weekly deadlines creates an urgency to complete the immediate assignments. As a result, graduate students often turn their attention to writing only after receiving a less than favorable grade on a written assignment or being given a faculty recommendation to improve writing; even then, graduate students usually address mechanical issues rather than the competencies needed to sustain long-term academic writing success.

The focus on writing increases across all disciplines towards the end of a graduate program since the graduate degree journey begins with coursework and ends with students independently writing a thesis or dissertation (Casanave and Hubbard 37, 44). Consequently, writing development tends to garner major attention by students, faculty and advisors at the final phase of advanced study. Graduate students willingly seek writing assistance or have faculty who recommend hiring professional editors while completing the final written project.

However, the skills needed to write an independent scholarly project take time to master, so waiting until late in a graduate program to develop these skills places students at a severe disadvantage while increasing pressure to perform in a short period of time. Academic writing involves analyzing, synthesizing and organizing information from multiple research based sources; it is the result of effectively intertwining critical thinking and critical reading to produce critical writing. When graduate students wait to cultivate these skills until they are absolutely needed, they face the burden of applying new strategies and shedding old habits in a foreign educational context.

During the first two stages of advanced study (coursework and comprehensive exams), graduate students do not have to work independently for a sustained period of time like they do during the final phase of study. Furthermore, the final writing project is approached, completed and assessed differently than class assignments or comprehensive exams, so graduate students struggle to complete it. This reality is further exacerbated by the loss of a structured classroom environment with the constant accountability of defined assignments, impending deadlines and weekly faculty contact.

With no classes to attend, no peers to interact with regularly and no professor imposing deadlines, late-stage graduate students understandably feel isolated, stressed and abandoned. Key initial steps, like identifying an appropriate research topic, become major obstacles to productivity during this final stage. As a result, graduate students are likely to waste valuable months engaged in fruitless activities; then, they become discouraged when their thesis or dissertation committee chair advises them to begin anew due to the lack of a worthy research topic, invalid research support or some other reason.

Nari Carter conducted research to improve her writing while a doctoral student; she published her findings in a review of literature on graduate student writing, pinpointing the following five writing challenges for students (408):

> **Common Graduate Student Writing Issues**
>
> 1. Tend to make mechanical and structural errors
> 2. Lack confidence and authority in their writing
> 3. Struggle to formulate arguments or theses supported by evidence
> 4. Experience difficulty responding to critiques of written work
> 5. Experience difficulty thinking and writing like scholars

Though numerous writing challenges exist at each stage of graduate study, they can be overcome.

Address Writing Issues Early

Since becoming a proficient academic writer is a development process (Carter 419), graduate students should focus on writing as early in their programs as possible (Bair and Mader 10; Mullen 125; Sallee, Hallett and Tierney 70). The blame for the widespread writing struggles of graduate students is placed at various levels. Some scholars fault departments, graduate programs and disciplinary specific curriculum for not including courses that teach graduate students the genre of research writing (Bair and Mader 10; Mullen 117; Ondrusek 185). Some scholars believe graduate level faculty should be trained to assess writing and mentor students (Mullen 125).

By far, most of the blame for academic writing ills rests upon graduate students. Once graduate students recognize that most faculty members, administrators and advisors point to writing deficiency within students, they will understand that the onus is placed on them to become proficient scholarly writers (Badenhorst et al. 1). Since the writing challenges of graduate students are not overwhelmingly perceived to stem from the institution, they are not addressed at the university level (Badenhorst et al. 3). Graduate faculty and administrators expect individual students who struggle with writing to obtain the help they need. Therefore, graduate students should seek assistance to develop as scholarly writers as quickly as possible, ideally during or prior to their first semester of study.

The earlier graduate students commit to developing their writing, the better equipped they are to complete a thesis, dissertation or final major writing project. Focusing on writing during coursework can minimize the writing problems graduate students face later in their programs, when writing is essential to completing the degree. The need for doctoral students is even greater because of the continuing percentage of students who are "ABD" (all but dissertation) and never join the approximately 50% of doctoral candidates who are able to earn a PhD (Council of Graduate Schools).

Know Graduate Faculty Writing Expectations

One problem that hinders graduate student writing development is students expect to receive writing guidance, instruction and information from faculty members, yet professors assume that graduate students possess adequate research and writing skills that they either acquired as undergraduates or in other graduate courses (Nelson, Range and Rosss 376; Sallee, Hallett and Tierney 66, 72). Understandably, graduate programs have high writing standards for students (Ondrusek 176). Unfortunately, those standards typically go unmet because incoming and matriculating graduate students do not possess the type of skills needed to produce sound scholarly writing.

Most graduate students have not built upon the research writing knowledge they acquired as undergraduates in Composition I and Composition II. Therefore, they do not know how to effectively formulate arguments or support them with sufficient research (Carter 408; Sallee, Hallett and Tierney 67). Consequently, many graduate students feel uncertain about what professors require and hesitate to seek direction, knowing faculty members expect them to already know how to write academically. Meanwhile, faculty members remain frustrated by the writing submitted by students who have been admitted into advanced academic study.

Unbeknownst to students, graduate faculty members do not expect to have to provide writing instruction, so most professors do not assess written assignments with the goal of cultivating scholarly writing (Nelson, Range and Ross 376). Additionally, evaluating academic writing with the intent of improving it is time and labor intensive (Sallee, Hallett and Tierney 67). Most faculty members either lack the time to provide extensive feedback or have not been trained to do so, yet they recognize writing that does not meet academic standards. Consequently, professors tend to note problems but do not explain how to improve writing, refer students to other resources, use methods that were used on them as graduate students or utilize a "trial and error" system for giving quality writing feedback (Badenhorst et al. 3). Regardless of their response to less than desirable writing, most faculty members do not feel it is their responsibility to develop the scholarly writing of graduate students.

English professors Christine Casanave and Philip Hubbard conducted research on faculty perspectives of graduate student writing. They surveyed professors at Stanford University about the specific writing skills they believed doctoral students need to develop. Their goal was to conduct a study focused on doctoral students, which was lacking at the time, and determine whether native English speaking and non-native English speaking students struggle with the same writing issues. While much of the information they gained from their faculty questionnaires was valuable, one topic that provides great insight into faculty expectations of graduate writing is the rating of nine writing skills. The writing abilities described in Casanave and Pearson's study are presented in the chart below; graduate students would do well to recognize that their professors expect them to be proficient in these nine areas, as documented by graduate teaching faculty surveyed by Casanave and Pearson (37).

Important Writing Skills for Graduate Students to Master

1. Analyzing and critiquing ideas
2. Organizing arguments from several sources
3. Summarizing information from one source
4. Arguing persuasively
5. Describing a procedure
6. Describing an object or idea
7. Proposing a solution
8. Expressing oneself creatively
9. Synthesizing information from multiple sources

Respond to Graduate Faculty Writing Expectations

Graduate students react in numerous ways when confronted with the high writing standards of professors. These reactions include writing anxiety, despair, feelings of inadequacy, denial, regret for half-heartedly paying attention in former writing classes, anger towards the professor for critiquing so harshly, a desperate plea to resubmit the work, a strong reality check, a search for writing resources that can help, embarrassment regarding their perceived subpar writing abilities, confusion over how to meet standards and determination to improve academic writing. The last response is the best response!

Under the current structure of graduate education, the reality is graduate students most likely will not be taught how to meet academic writing standards at the institutional level. Few graduate programs offer scholarly writing courses and the already full curriculum does not have the flexibility to add courses (Badenhorst et al. 2; Sallee, Hallett and Tierney 67). Graduate level faculty typically lack the time, energy, and sometimes, the expertise to cultivate their students into scholarly writers. The reality is that regardless of who should bear the blame for writing problems, graduate students must assume responsibility for developing their ability to write at a scholarly level.

Writing is a craft full of techniques, approaches and principles. Though graduate students may be fortunate to have an academic writing or publication course offered in their program, encounter a professor committed to developing scholarly writing in students or acquire a committee chair with the desire, skill and time to cultivate the academic writing of their students, graduate students cannot rely on these avenues to improve their writing. When graduate students choose to proactively acquire the information, guidance and resources needed to hone their scholarly writing, they can successfully develop it.

Consider the Writing Center: A Traditional Scholarly Writing Resource

Students are often directed to the traditional campus-based writing center, which has evolved into writing studios and labs on some campuses, to overcome individual writing problems (Badenhorst et al. 4). From institution to institution, writing centers have differing ways of operating; they vary according to where they are housed, how they are funded, the students they serve, how large they are, the types of services they provide and the educational level of those who staff them (Hoon 48).

The varying functions of writing centers determine the value they provide to graduate students; often, the benefit depends on the particular needs of the student and the specific center and mission the center fulfills within the university. Writing centers are typically filled with ample English language resources, such as grammar hand-outs, writing skill workshop/seminar offerings and writing guides, to improve basic research writing. Since most centers offer individualized tutoring, graduate students can benefit from working with someone who has studied the English language and can pinpoint individual problem areas in grammar, style and organization. Most writing centers are designed to meet the needs of the most populous student at the university, the undergraduate, and are staffed by graduate students.

Many graduate students, specifically doctoral students, desire a degree-holder, rather than a peer, to help them become proficient scholarly writers. Additionally, writing centers have limited availability, especially during peak assignment times of the semester, because they service the entire university community; therefore, they (like faculty members) often cannot accommodate the intensive, ongoing writing needs of graduate students. Furthermore, writing center resources tend to focus on research papers, grammar and fundamental elements of argumentation.

Often, graduate students need more advanced and sustained writing supports than writing centers provide. However, before dismissing any institutional resource, graduate students should determine whether a writing center can meet their writing needs, especially if a faculty member advises them to utilize it. If writing center services are not beneficial, a graduate student should be able to articulate the reasons to a faculty member.

Recognize that Scholarly Writing Is More Than Writing

Understanding the culture of graduate school allows graduate students to situate writing in its proper context. Graduate school facilitates the academic growth of students in their researching, thinking and writing abilities (Ondrusek 180). By promoting progress in these areas, graduate study develops students into articulate, confident scholars who can make meaningful contributions to their field through ideas that are well developed and supported by valid research (Mullen 118). An isolated focus on writing hinders the holistic academic maturation needed because scholarly writing is intimately connected to other academic activities.

Successfully navigating graduate study requires a mental adjustment. One of the main shifts has to do with how graduate students perceive themselves and their writing abilities (Mullen 120). Most graduate students, especially those in non-writing based disciplines, do not consider themselves to be writers. However, graduate students first must embrace the identity of a scholarly writer if they expect to align with the purpose of graduate education and understand the interconnectedness of the academic activities they perform in graduate school.

Shed the Undergraduate Mentality About Education and Writing

Undergraduate education includes academic activities, such as attending class, reading textbooks and taking exams, as well as non-academic activities, like enjoying a social life. Within the academic realm, writing has a place but typically does not dominate undergraduate education. The non-academic realm is filled with extracurricular activities, such as Greek life, athletics and cultural events. Campus is the proverbial oyster for a traditional undergraduate student with a flexible class schedule, financial aid, scholarship money and independence from parents to explore it all.

Instead of a non-academic life filled with extracurricular activities, non-traditional undergraduate students often have the responsibilities of working, raising a family and/or trying to maintain a semblance of life normalcy as they balance multiple roles. The undergraduate experience for the non-traditional student is filled with years of sacrifices, sleepless nights, juggling competing priorities and a determination to finish. Academics is one part of the multi-faceted life of an undergraduate student, whether the status of that student is traditional or non-traditional.

Students at the undergraduate level have a divided perspective of academic life inside the classroom and non academic life outside of the classroom. Many undergraduate classes, even the courses within a declared major, are considered a necessary part of obtaining the ultimate goal: a degree to progress to the next stage of life. Most undergraduate students do not develop the habit of attending professors' office hours or interacting with faculty members outside of class. Many undergraduate students do not collaborate with classmates until assigned group work or faced with an urgent need to join a study group to pass an exam.

In regards to writing, most undergrads do not register for writing courses beyond the required first year composition courses unless an interest or major is connected to writing. Therefore, the approach to writing for many undergraduates is rather lackadaisical; they write to meet assignment guidelines. Undergraduate students become adept at conducting research and writing a research paper that is properly cited to avoid being accused of plagiarism. Upon graduation, most undergraduates envision a life free of researching a topic, writing a paper and citing sources. The percentage of undergraduate students who become graduate students, either shortly after earning a bachelor's degree or sometime later, cannot expect to succeed in the familiar setting of higher education with a dichotomous approach to classroom and non-classroom activities.

Make a Mental Paradigm Shift

To be successful in graduate education, graduate students must adopt a new way of viewing education, information and themselves (Ondrusek 180). Though undergraduate and graduate students are serviced at the same institution, they are not educated the same, evaluated the same or treated the same. Graduate students, through graduate programs, enter a different realm of the university. Therefore, graduate students do not have the luxury of enjoying a segregated educational life as many undergraduates. In fact, the opposite is expected of the graduate student: most of the activities outside of the classroom should complement work in the classroom so that academic and non-academic life are fully integrated. Additionally, writing is an integral aspect of graduate study in every department, not an ancillary part.

Faculty expectations differ for undergraduate and graduate students. Graduate faculty do not give everything to their students in the form of instructions, guidance and deadlines. So, a passive learning approach is not beneficial for graduate study. Rather than constantly needing guidance, instruction and explanation from professors and advisors, graduate students are expected to take the initiative to build upon their undergraduate educational foundation.

Graduate study can be likened to a training program, and graduate students are better identified as scholars in training. Faculty members do not view graduate students as only students; they also see them as burgeoning professionals. As trainees, graduate students are expected to think, act and write like a scholar, or "a learned or erudite person, especially one who has a profound knowledge of a particular subject" (American Heritage 652). A scholar possesses an advanced level of knowledge; in the context of higher education, graduate students need to know the culture of higher education and their particular discipline.

Graduate students should know how to research, write, study and engage in an academic discipline based upon the educational process they completed to earn a bachelor's and/or master's degree.

As a place of academic training, graduate school holds numerous expectations for its scholars in training, whether explicitly articulated or not by the graduate school, college, department, faculty or advisors. Fulfilling these expectations requires graduate students to commit to integrating their personal, educational and professional lives. Listed below are some of the expectations faculty members, advisors and administrators have of graduate students. To meet these expectations, graduate students must adopt a certain way of thinking.

Expectations of Graduate Students

- Take a critical approach to thinking, reading and writing.
- Become active participants in professional organizations and at professional conferences.
- Know and read academic journals pertinent to their field and research interests.
- Work cooperatively, without complaint, with classmates on assignments, papers and presentations, professionally resolving any obstacles that arise.
- Be comfortable speaking and presenting publicly (and be able to do so spontaneously).
- Seek out and invest in institutional and non-institutional resources that help to develop any area needed.
- Adjust gracefully to shifting course or program assignments, projects and deadlines.
- Develop relationships with professors, classmates and colleagues beyond the classroom.
- Read, analyze and create scholarship.

CHAPTER | 2

Become a Scholar

Graduate school is designed to equip students to engage fully in what it means to be a scholar. The abilities to produce, articulate and disseminate scholarship in writing are the distinguishing characteristics of a scholar. Scholars inquire into past and current information (research and read), generate new knowledge (think), organize evidence (think and write) and share their findings within and outside of their field (write and present). The goal of scholars is to produce meaningful scholarship based on their research interests; their scholarship has various forms, including novel research studies, best practices, journal articles and conference papers.

Scholars are adept in generating scholarship in numerous ways; however, each way requires an ability to write at an advanced level (Ondrusek 185). The distinct genre of scholarly writing is demanding, intensive and laborious. Therefore, graduate students, whether experienced business writers, great reflective writers or skilled creative writers, must commit to developing the competencies needed to produce writing that requires significant planning and thinking. The ultimate purpose for creating scholarship is to have it reviewed, judged and shared with a larger academic community. When graduate students understand the expectations for scholars, they can view every course, assignment and interaction with others in academia as part of their preparation for joining a community of scholars.

Learn the Academic Conversation

Beyond their affiliations with local academic departments and universities, graduate students are expected to connect to the larger academic community. All scholarly writing is positioned within a "collective" body of written works (Carter 409). Though graduate students individually write about topics that interest them, as scholars, they are expected to write with an awareness of the larger academic community within which their research subjects are situated; this community is known as a "discourse community" (Badenhorst et al. 4; Carter 419; Wisker 65). In more familiar terms, graduate students are joining an ongoing written "conversation" every time they engage in scholarly writing (Wisker 73).

Learning the appropriate academic conversation within a disciplinary community is an important expectation of budding scholars. To effectively write within an academic community, graduate students first must fully understand the conversation. The two terms used to refer to the academic conversation, or body of written works within a discourse community, are scholarship and literature. These terms refer to the books, articles, reviews, manuscripts and other academic works pertaining to a research subject; they are the documents created that form the conversation within an academic, or discourse, community. As scholars in training, graduate students are expected to constantly read the literature pertaining to their declared research interests within a discourse community. The goal of such voracious reading is to become intimately acquainted with the full academic conversation, past and present. While reading the literature, graduate students should note the subjects, subtopics, trends, nuances, threads and contributors to the ongoing academic conversation. Pinpointing then understanding an academic conversation requires significant dedication to researching and reading, so graduate students are expected to be diligent, patient and strategic in reading the literature within a particular discourse community.

The timeframe for learning an academic conversation depends on the specific discipline, sub-specialty and research interest(s) of a graduate student. Some scholarly conversations extend back hundreds of years so the literature is rather extensive while other discourse communities are newly formed; therefore, the extent of their academic conversation is not as vast. However, the focus of a budding scholar is not simply on learning the scholarship of a discourse community as quickly as possible but on closely reading the scholarship to gain a thorough understanding of the history, dynamics and voices of the conversation. An example of an actual doctoral student's journey in learning a discourse community is provided in the appendix.

Read Scholarship Critically

In order to meet graduate program expectations, incoming graduate students should focus on improving their critical reading and critical thinking abilities, which is part of academic literacy. Though much of the academic literacy literature focuses on undergraduates (Badenhorst et al. 2), it is important for graduate students to learn the relationship between reading, thinking critically and developing an academic identity (Bair and Mader 2; McAlpine 359). Critical reading and critical thinking are two sides of the same academic coin because critical reading cannot be achieved without constant critical thinking, which is analyzing and synthesizing information. In graduate study, the information to analyze is the scholarship within a discourse community.

Scholarship shows that graduate students devote as much time to reading as they do to writing; therefore, they should learn to read "strategically" (McAlpine 352-353). When reading scholarship, graduate students are expected to carefully examine what they are reading in order to grasp the relationship of the content within an individual document to other literature within the academic conversation. Reading for comprehension is one level of reading. Beyond understanding what they read, graduate students need to be able to question what they read.

To read critically, graduate students should engage with the text as if conversing with the author. If discourse communities are better understood as written academic conversations, an individual document within the community represents one voice of the conversation.

Therefore, graduate students can engage with the words they are reading as if the author is speaking those words. When budding scholars read ideas, methods or concepts they do not understand, they can highlight them or note so in the margins. If graduate students have questions to clarify confusion or misunderstanding, they can pose them on the document. If graduate students agree with a point, they can state why. If graduate students believe the author has drawn a hasty conclusion, made a generalization and/or presented insufficient evidence, they can explain why. Instead of engaging with the author verbally, scholars engage with an author of a written source through thoughts and notes when reading. Refer to the appendix for an actual doctoral student's experience learning academic literacy practices.

Objectivity and openness are essential traits for reading critically because scholars must be open to modifying their positions. As graduate students explore answers to their questions on a subject, the answers they discover in a text may challenge their thoughts. The responses may lead them down a new path of discovering information they may not have considered. Or, the answers may shed light on aspects of the conversation with which the scholar once disagreed. Objectivity and openness during critical reading allow scholars' positions on a subject to evolve as they delve deeply into an academic conversation.

Graduate scholars also should utilize critical thinking while reading to determine how individual pieces of scholarship within an academic conversation interact with one another. As graduate students analyze complex ideas, theories, methods or research to pinpoint important relationships among and between them, they can consider how the information is related to other literature they have read within the academic conversation. Evaluating content from multiple sources within the literature allows graduate students to synthesize the information in dynamic ways. As graduate students become more knowledgeable about an academic community, they are able to contribute to the conversation in insightful ways.

Advice from Seasoned Graduate Students

- *Improve reading and writing skills, participate in seminars and write everyday.*
- *Use every assignment to write about your topic or research interest.*
- *Cultivate relationships with your professors.*
- *Be involved with people doing similar research and consider new areas to apply research ideas.*
- *Engage in classes, workshops, etc. to prepare you before you enter a program.*
- *Do research about resources outside of the academic program.*
- *Participate in programs and seminars (you may be surprised by what you don't know and the help available).*
- *Integrate fully into the graduate school community for they will understand the highs and lows, especially encouraging you when you feel defeated.*

> ▶ *Read the Program-specific handbook early.*
> ▶ *Start with the end in mind by creating a 5 year plan.*
> ▶ *Never stop reading! Not only does it help you to develop your research plan but it also helps you to learn writing styles in your field.*
> ▶ *Before enrolling, talk to the graduate students already in the program to learn about faculty and the department atmosphere.*
> ▶ *Attend conferences during your first year.*

Develop an Authoritative Scholarly Voice

When asked to write about or within a discourse community, graduate students easily can be overwhelmed, especially if recently introduced to an academic conversation. Graduate students can feel as if they are simply stating information they have read in the literature instead of contributing any original ideas, which is understandable. Until scholars become knowledgeable about the various aspects of an academic conversation, they will not be confident inserting themselves into the scholarship. Though learning the literature about a topic requires time, graduate students are expected to be able to write about scholarship, or develop a research voice, during their first year of study.

The struggle of graduate students to develop an authentic research voice is well documented (Ondrusek 181-182; Wisker 66). However, this challenge naturally decreases as graduate students gain increased knowledge of a disciplinary community with each article they read, course they take and idea they generate. With a grasp of the history, voices and shifts of an academic conversation, graduate students begin to notice omissions, assumptions and oversights, commonly known as gaps, in the scholarship based on their questions about selected theories, methods and claims. Through this process, graduate students enter the realm of academic inquiry and begin to create knowledge based on the information they have analyzed. The new approaches, thoughts and applications that graduate students conceive mark the emergence of their unique academic voice.

Improve Critical Reading and Critical Thinking

Once graduate students engage in academic inquiry, the type of critical reading and thinking they conduct evolves. They start to note the styles of writing within their academic community so that they can begin to absorb and model them when sharing their research ideas. With a clear scholarly identity, graduate students read to intentionally study how academic topics within their discourse community are written about, organized and supported. Through critical reading, graduate students learn acceptable and effective methods for writing about theory, challenging established ideas in writing, presenting methodology and composing original thoughts about academic subjects.

Thus, the same critical thinking principles utilized to understand the scholarship within an academic community when reading critically are needed to write ideas clearly. When graduate students can critically read and think effectively about literature in the field of study, they then apply those same skills to construct well researched and supported arguments. Regular composition of research-based arguments helps graduate students meet the professional expectation to think, read and write as scholarly authorities who are clear about their unique contributions to a discourse community.

Embrace the Scholar's Responsibility to Write

Graduate school, as a scholarly training program, assists graduate students in developing a research identity and voice. With a clear research voice, graduate students can fulfill their professional responsibilities to publish (Mullen 119). As part of an academic conversation, scholarship is for sharing with the discourse community, not hoarding. Successful scholars not only intimately know their subject areas but have perfected distributing their specialized knowledge to a large, and sometimes varied, audience. Therefore, graduate students are expected to disseminate research via writing for scholarly publication and presenting at professional conferences (Carter 408; Ondrusek 178).

Graduate programs give graduate students the opportunity to engage in producing scholarship in various forms. Depending on their academic discipline, graduate students will be expected to compose scholarship throughout their coursework; some of those ways include critical summaries, non-critical summaries, brief research papers, long research papers, seminar papers, lab reports, group-based writing, literature reviews, case studies and position papers (Casanave and Hubbard 36).

Prepare for the Scholarly Rite of Passage

During the last phase of advanced study, graduate students experience an educational rite of passage that marks their formal transition from student to scholar through a ceremony where students orally defend a comprehensive writing project. The comprehensive project, known as a dissertation at the doctoral level and thesis at the master's level, is the culmination of a student's ability to develop a research voice.

Through the final project, students demonstrate that they have mastered the complex, integrated skills of researching, critically reading scholarship, critically thinking about literature, developing an authentic research voice and critically writing within an established discourse community. The final project also proves that the scholar in training has been trained sufficiently by veteran faculty members to produce valuable scholarship.

For the oral defense, which is the title of the ceremony, graduate scholars condense the scholarship contained within the final project into a presentation and formally present it to a committee of faculty members. After the presentation, graduate students field questions from the committee regarding their research. The final writing project and its oral defense demonstrate that a graduate student can translate information to other professional academicians in a coherent, organized educated manner, in writing and orally.

The scholarly rite of passage ceremony continues after the presentation. After the committee finishes questioning the graduate student, the committee asks the candidate to leave the room while committee members discuss the research, dissertation or thesis and its oral defense. Once the committee has completed its discussion and is satisfied with the caliber of work presented, the committee chair opens the door and invites the master's or doctoral student to re-enter the room, noting the official transition from graduate student to professional scholar. At the PhD level, this transition is further solidified by the committee chair addressing the candidate as "Dr." when requesting that the scholar enter the room.

The committee may require changes to the written project, which is a formality for the scholar to complete. However, the student has earned the degree after successfully defending his or her research orally. The university awards the degree during the generally scheduled commencement ceremony after the newly minted scholar makes any needed changes to the final written project and submits it to the graduate school for final approval. For doctoral level scholars, the final aspect of the rite of passage occurs during the graduation ceremony. At the ceremony, the committee chair hoods the new PhD with designated doctoral regalia as the scholar's name is announced. The hooding and special regalia mark the scholar's admission into the PhD ranks.

The necessity of writing development across all graduate programs to traverse this scholarly rite of passage successfully is indisputable. Whether in Humanities, Social Sciences, Health, Business or Science, Technology,

Engineering and Math (STEM) fields, writing that reflects a sophisticated level of reading, researching and thinking remains vital to earning an advanced degree. While some disciplines introduce academic writing assignments immediately, others do not emphasize writing until later in the program because they focus on research methods and theoretical application early in the program. Regardless of when the expectation is placed on graduate students to write at a higher level, scholarly writing development remains integral to earning a graduate degree.

Dissertation Advice from Doctoral Candidates

> ▶ *Seek input of those around you when choosing committee members and understand relationships among committee members you choose.*
> ▶ *Have a clear idea of the role the advisor or chair should play. Never stop reading! Not only does it help you to develop your research plan but it also helps you to learn writing styles in your field.*
> ▶ *Start planning for the dissertation at the earlier stages of the program; the most important advice is to have a solid plan.*
> ▶ *Love your dissertation topic; it should be something you really want to see come to fruition.*
> ▶ *Know the research areas of all committee members.*
> ▶ *Meet with your advisor regularly and put in writing what you agree to do each time you meet.*
> ▶ *Communicate regularly with your major chair.*

> ▶ *Take notes and record advisor meetings (follow up in email to document important info, action items, any changes in direction); save all emails and keep copies of all records.*
> ▶ *Be sure to know your major professor well.*

Expect to Write Beyond the Degree

Graduate students who embrace the responsibility of developing a scholarly writing identity early on are better equipped to matriculate through graduate study. Writing is not needed simply to earn a passing grade, complete a professor's assignment or write a thesis or dissertation. Writing is needed to become a successful scholar, while enrolled in a graduate program and after graduation (Carter 408; Mullen 118; Ondrusek 185).

After a graduate student earns a degree, scholarly writing abilities are critical to professional success, whether needed for grants and other forms of research funding, tenure and promotion, publication of research or increased job responsibilities. Those who enter academic departments as faculty members will never shed their duty as scholarly writers. Those with an applied graduate degree will retain a scholarly writing identity to varying degrees and for various time periods, depending on their position.

Regardless of the career objective, the professional expectation is that any person with a graduate degree can write at a scholarly level. So, whether advanced degree holders remain in academia or pursue non-academic careers, they will be expected to think, write and research in a way that those lacking a graduate degree cannot. The question is, "Are you ready to embrace your scholarly responsibility to write?"

CHAPTER | 3

Develop a Systematic Approach to Writing

One of the most vital aspects of producing solid scholarly writing is having an organized approach to writing. Academic writing should and can be strategic, not haphazard. Once graduate students apply the proper steps to produce sound, polished writing, they can organize their research and ideas into coherent, clear writing.

Understand the Writing Process

Students educated in the United States have been exposed to the writing process repeatedly. More important than knowing the stages of the writing process is understanding the actions that eliminate counterproductive behaviors and reduce anxiety, frustration and stress related to an unstructured approach to writing.

While many students claim to work best under pressure, the fact remains that strong writing results from utilizing a process that allows for distinct activities to occur over a period of time. Typically, students produce under pressure because they no longer can afford to procrastinate due to an impending deadline. Research shows that academic writing requires multiple revisions (Nelson, Range and Ross 376; Ondrusek 183; Sallee, Hallett and Tierney 70), a process that cannot occur when a graduate student procrastinates and writes under pressure.

The traditional writing process has four stages, which are prewriting, drafting, revising and editing. However, not every writer needs a four-step writing process; some scholars use more steps while others utilize fewer. The goal is to know the value and purpose of distinct activities that occur at each stage. With this understanding, graduate students can develop a personalized approach to writing that suits them based on each step in the traditional writing process.

When applied to academic writing, the four stages of the writing process are recursive rather than linear, which means writers can expect to move fluidly through the stages rather than completing step one, then step two, then step three, then step four. In fact, graduate students likely will revisit a previous stage at some point later in the process. Therefore, graduate students should remain open, anticipating the need to return to stage one or two during the final stages of the process. In order to move fluidly through the stages of the writing process, graduate students must understand them.

Stage One: Prewrite

Prewriting is everything that occurs before formal writing begins. Many people do not realize that the physical act of writing is only one part of the writing process. The first stage of the writing process, known as prewriting, allows scholars to clarify their thoughts about a topic and the accompanying research. Unfortunately, many graduate students write too soon. When ideas are jumbled and have not been sorted out properly, the writing reflects the cluttered state of the mind. Therefore, writers should think and plan before they draft.

Because people need a way to organize their ideas before they begin to write, prewriting is such a critical stage of the writing process. When done properly, prewriting reduces disorganization and incoherence in a document. Prewriting includes gathering adequate research about the topic, sifting through research sources and carefully reading the research about the topic.

The research based nature of academic writing requires scholars to gather ample research, which is a valuable academic skill to master. Securing research involves scouring databases for valid research, reading abstracts, skimming the literature, selecting useful sources and organizing those sources, activities which can be extremely time consuming. Graduate students should be efficient in conducting academic research; librarians and research workshops are excellent resources for informing and guiding scholars in the details of accessing databases, limiting searches, identifying the right key terms, conducting advanced searches and other techniques for acquiring information. When researching, scholars need a clear sense of what they know about the topic, yet they also need to remain open regarding what they need to discover about the topic from an academic perspective.

Once graduate students select the final sources, they must read them critically, not simply for comprehension. As discussed in the second chapter, it is imperative for graduate students to allow critical reading and critical thinking to precede their writing. Together, graduate students' critical reading and thinking ensure that they have fully analyzed and understood research sources before the formal writing stage. By critically thinking during the prewriting stage, graduate scholars can clarify the various relationships, information and concepts they have read while researching. Once they have clarified these aspects of the research, graduate students can organize their thoughts in a logical, sequential manner. When graduate students do not complete these academic activities, the writing that results is a hodgepodge of everything they have read.

Consider Audience

Certain questions need to be answered in the prewriting stage. One central question to answer is "Who is the audience for whom the writing is geared?" All effective communication, including writing, is audience-driven so graduate scholars must write purposefully for their audiences because an audience dictates the organizational and stylistic choices a writer makes. An audience determines which ideas need to be relayed and in what fashion; therefore, a writer should give thoughtful consideration to what the audience knows about a subject, needs to know about a subject, feels about a subject and wants to learn about a subject.

Different audiences possess varying levels of knowledge, assumptions and beliefs about the same information. Consider the varied approaches of writing for the following audiences: veteran faculty members; a group of practitioners; the editor of a highly respected journal; classmates; a combination of experts and non-experts attending a conference; a panel of administrators who administer research funding. Decisions regarding information to include, such as the amount of discipline-specific jargon, the type of examples and the organization of content, would not be the same for each of these audiences. Some would require a great amount of explanation before being presented with the first point while others would be bored if given a detailed history on the topic.

Additionally, graduate scholars should recognize that their academic audience is layered. When submitting assignments for courses, students sometimes mistakenly think of the individual professor as the sole audience. However, every faculty member represents a working professional in the field. The professor also could be a journal editor, officer of a prominent professional organization, conference panel organizer or a prolific researcher, author or grant writer seeking contributors to his or her book or grant project. Therefore, every opportunity to write during graduate study should be viewed with a keen awareness of the larger professional audience and multiple roles each reader could be fulfilling. With the audience at the forefront of their minds when prewriting, graduate scholars can select and organize information needed for their particular audience.

35

Pinpoint a Primary Purpose

Another question to consider during the prewriting stage is the intent for writing; authors must decide whether their main goal is to inform, persuade or entertain an audience. Once scholars select a primary purpose for writing, they can choose the appropriate method for presenting information. For example, when a scholar's primary purpose is to inform about a topic, he or she does not need to utilize as many strategies as when persuading. Persuasion, also known as argumentation, is approached much more strategically than informative writing.

Usually, scholars write with different purposes throughout a document; however, before beginning to write, they should pinpoint one primary purpose for the entire document. For example, a scholar attempting to persuade an audience about the validity of a research study may need to devote three-fourths of the space to sharing information so that the audience has adequate background information to follow the argument. Then, the scholar can spend the last one-fourth of the space convincing the audience of the value and benefits of the study. By answering questions about audience and purpose during the prewriting stage, graduate scholars have a clear sense of why they are writing and for whom they are writing.

Compose a Working Thesis

The central position a scholar asserts in a document is articulated in the thesis. Therefore, the thesis is known as the central idea of a written work; it contains the main point, claim or argument a writer makes. Though the thesis may change as graduate scholars continue the research and writing processes, they need to identify a working thesis, or a tentative central idea, during the prewriting stage to ensure that they have something meaningful to state about a topic that can be supported. A writer can compose the thesis at any point during the prewriting stage: as early as the research gathering stage or later when employing one of the prewriting techniques described in the next section.

Every academic writing project, whether a 10-page book review, 25-page conference paper or 200-page dissertation, needs a central idea that is expressed in, ideally, one sentence but no more than two sentences. A working thesis should be broad enough that it encompasses all of the evidence, support and information that will be included in the document. Only after graduate scholars have a clear sense of their overarching statement, position or argument about a subject can they successfully draft a working thesis. Once crafted, a working thesis determines which information, research and ideas to include in the document. The thesis may be refined or solidified during a later stage of the writing process.

Writing a solid thesis statement is a craft; the thesis should be specific, but not too narrow. It must be broad enough to allow for the development of the main idea but cannot be so encompassing that it does not limit the topic sufficiently. Thesis statements are tailored to one's topic, so they must suit the scope, nature and evidence that an author has gathered. A sample thesis statement is included in one of the prewriting techniques described in the following pages.

Utilize Prewriting Techniques

Writing occurs during the prewriting stage but not in a formal fashion. The purpose of writing during the prewriting stage is for writers to bring focus and structure to research ideas and thoughts about a subject, not to actually write about the topic. Prewriting techniques are the options available to graduate scholars for organizing their ideas and research; these techniques ensure scholars have considered their ideas thoroughly before writing. The prewriting strategies listed in the chart below are described in detail for the next few pages and graduate scholar examples of most strategies are provided.

Prewriting Techniques	
1. Annotating	5. Questioning
2. Brainstorming	6. Discussing
3. Free Writing	7. Outlining
4. Clustering	8. Journaling

Annotate

Annotating is the act of summarizing the major ideas in a document in approximately one-fourth the length of the original source. An annotation captures the most salient points of a document rather than all of the details, supports and information. However, graduate students should use discretion when annotating lengthier sources because the purpose of the annotation is to capture the main ideas, not to have a certain length.

Annotations are valuable as a prewriting technique for several reasons. For one, they require a careful reading of sources for significance so they often help the writer of the annotation to comprehend significant principles, tenets and evidence. Writing annotations also helps to develop critical reading skills because writers read with the goal of pinpointing the central idea and key sub-points. By annotating sources, scholars become skilled in fleshing out the most salient points of a source when reading.

Annotations are written in a particular format, which gives structure to the ideas of a source and forces graduate scholars to eliminate unnecessary information ruminating in their heads. Annotations should not be written in chronological order of the original source. This approach is only effective if the author of the source begins with the central thesis and leads to the main sub-points. However, many authors do not present their ideas in that order, especially when presenting arguments. The first line of an annotation should identify the author's main point, which is not necessarily the first point made in the document. Then, the author's main sub-points are listed, including any noteworthy, compelling or critical evidence used as support. So, a graduate scholar must critically read to determine the central position and main points, no matter where they are located in a document.

Writing annotations is preferred to using abstracts to remember sources and have long-term value for graduate scholars. For one, though abstracts summarize sources, not all abstracts are written well or describe an author's central position. Additionally, graduate scholars can highlight particular information present in a source but not referenced in an abstract. Graduate students can only acquire some information by reading then annotating a source. Writing annotations is especially vital to graduate scholars as a means of building a personal catalogue of scholarship surrounding their research interests.

Graduate scholars can write two types of annotations: objective and evaluative. The evaluative annotation is an objective annotation with additional sentences devoted to describing the strengths and weaknesses of the sources, the author's assessment of certain aspects of the source and/or the relevancy of the source to the scholar's research interests.

Graduate scholars may be interested in certain methodologies, theoretical frameworks, case studies or research references in the source and can note that particular information in an evaluative annotation. Or, scholars can indicate how they anticipate utilizing the source in connection with their research. Though some articles seem unforgettable when first read, graduate scholars read hundreds, if not thousands, of pages of scholarship over the course of their degree programs. A personal catalogue of evaluative annotations allows graduate scholars to reference sources from their first semester or early year(s) in the program years. The sample annotation below ends with a few evaluative sentences noting the significance of the source to the writer's interests.

Example of an Evaluative Annotation

In this article, McAlpine explores the pivotal but often overlooked role that reading has "in the development of student thinking, writing and academic identity" of graduate students (351). McAlphine based her findings on a longitudinal study of work of social science and STEM students in Canada and the UK, including their academic habits and daily experiences in their programs. The article pinpoints the issues related to reading, benefits of reading as well as the different purposes for which social science and STEM students read. The article notes that institutions should acknowledge the value of reading as an intellectual "developmental learning process" for graduate students; it provides specific recommendations for helping students to become more intentional, active agents when reading (357). McAlpine also delineates the ways in which reading acclimates students to a body of research and helps them join the broader scholarly community.

This article is useful because it clearly articulates problems, needs and gaps of scholarly development at the institutional and individual level. Additionally, it is useful for determining the types of writing services that need to be developed to service institutions and/or their graduate students, specifically in terms of the value of incorporating reading and its value into developing the academic abilities of graduate students.

Brainstorm/List

Brainstorming, which is very similar to listing, is a prewriting technique used to uncover all of the potential ideas and information writers have about a subject. Listing is a little more formal than brainstorming because ideas are organized in word, phrase and/or clause form whereas any format is acceptable when brainstorming. The goal of brainstorming and listing is to explore all possible angles about a topic without filtering ideas through judgments about the usefulness, worthiness or relevancy of the information. The example below utilizes listing to explore possible topics based on research completed about an academic subject.

Example of Listing to Select a Topic

- *Similarities and differences between the Culture of Honor in Islamic communities, small Mediterranean communities and the American South*
- *The role Honor, Shame and Pride have in promoting violence within a Culture of Honor*
- *Why men use violence to protect their reputation: forms of disrespect and the male response to it*
- *A culture of honor can develop in any community where there are scarce resources and the isolation of people competing for those resources (i.e. inner city)*
- *The gendered nature of Honor Killings: violence against women, committed by men in order to defend their family's "honor" (based on cultural anthropology: Islamic communities and small, Mediterranean communities)*
- *A version of "culture of honor" exists in the South (according to social psychologists), only violence in the name of honor usually committed by men against men, such as dueling, but also against women in the home (domestic violence)*

Free write

Free writing is a prewriting technique that is also beneficial for overcoming writer's block. Free writing is the act of writing uninterrupted for a period of time; it is a forced activity when used for overcoming writer's block. When free writing, writers set a small period of time, usually no longer than five minutes, and write continuously about ideas that come to mind during the time period. Once the clock starts, writing or typing must occur, even if the writer initially draws a blank; a person can state "I don't know what to write," but he or she has to write something rather than sitting and thinking. The same statement can be written repeatedly until a different thought emerges. The forced writing usually gets the mind so focused that ideas are released, immediately or eventually.

Free writing is an excellent strategy for removing all of the ideas about a topic from one's mind. When free writing, a person literally dumps information onto paper or a computer screen with no regard for flow, organization or grammar. The free writing example below was conducted in preparation for a doctoral level course assignment.

Example of Free Writing

The role of compulsory K-12 education as being liberating or oppressive depends on many variables with race and gender leading the list of circumstances that change the opinion. Education is not equally administered for reasons of racial bias that set standards of pedagogy, assessments, curriculum and opportunities according to the labels that define the rate of success for a group of individuals. Because of education's "one size fits all" design that ignores diverse cultures represented in classrooms, the ability to achieve liberation through authentic self-development for children is diminished. Instead education becomes a means to assimilate a community classified as "other" through processes such as irrelevant content, lack of differentiated instruction and low expectations. The liberating nature of education is buried under bureaucratic frameworks supported by racism, misconceptions of best practices and less than helpful educational policies. Therefore, education represents both freedom and oppression to certain people because of the way it was designed to advance one group.

Cluster/Map

Clustering, also known as mapping, is a useful prewriting technique for graduate scholars who like to visually depict their thoughts. Similar ideas are grouped, or clustered, then connected with other ideas according to a significant relationship identified by the writer. The main ideas are placed in circles, squares or some other shape; then similar ideas are either situated in the same location and/or connected through lines. When clustering, writers literally map their ideas in an organized way on to a paper, board or computer screen. Below is an example of the visual mapping of ideas

Question

Questioning takes a journalistic approach to organizing ideas by asking pointed questions about ideas and research. When questioning, writers ask the five "W's" (who, what, when, where and why) about their subject as well as the one "H" (how) in order to pinpoint the saliency of their ideas. This prewriting technique ensures that the writer of the topic has a global perspective that can be supported and developed further. The writer can make this technique as broad or detailed as needed. The focus of the questions can be changed based upon the topic, audience and particular context of the research. Additional questions based upon the main questions can be posed to delve deeper into ideas about the topic. The example below provides the beginning questions of probing one's ideas about a subject that has been researched.

Example of Questioning to Consider Possible Angles for a Topic

1. What is the motivation for promoting IB Schools in the US and specifically in urban areas?
2. Who are the external influencers affecting US IB programs' organizational structure?
3. How does the US alignment of the IB program in urban schools mirror the designed purpose?
4. When is the IB program a good fit for urban schools?
5. Why do US administrators weakly enforce the IBO World goal established in the IB framework?
6. Where are IB schools concentrated in the US?

Discuss

Discussion allows a writer to engage others in conversation regarding their ideas about a subject. Typically, thoughts are clarified when expressed, whether in a written or spoken form. Discussing is the only prewriting technique that does not involve writing though it is beneficial for a writer to take notes based on the conversation. Graduate scholars can choose to discuss their ideas with individuals or small groups. The role of the discussant is to probe the writer about his or her ideas. The discussants can be knowledgeable or uniformed about the topic. Sometimes, it is useful for the discussant to be informed about the topic in order to achieve true clarity of thought; sometimes, it is better for the discussant to be unfamiliar with the subject.

When utilizing this prewriting strategy, a writer can decide to get varied perspectives, from the informed to the uninformed. Regardless of the number or knowledge level of the discussants, the goal of discussing is for writers to engage in dialogue that allows them to meaningfully express, explore and question their thoughts on a topic. The clarifying questions asked, the knowledge level of the discussant(s) and the time available to converse determine the extent of the conversation. An example of discussing is not provided since this prewriting strategy is oral in nature.

Outline

Outlining is a familiar form of prewriting to graduate scholars because it is usually the prewriting technique encouraged in educational settings. An outline records main ideas, sub-points and supporting evidence about a topic in a logical order using numbers or Roman numerals. The ideas can be written in word form, phrase form, sentence form or a combination of forms.

Many mathematical/logical thinkers and educators prefer outlines because they not only organize ideas but also provide the order in which ideas are presented. However, outlining is not the most effective form of organizing ideas for everyone. The outline below organizes ideas according to the sections explained in a doctoral level course assignment; it is a combination outline that includes words, phrases and sentences.

Example of Outlining to Organize Research and Ideas

Topic: Academic Coaching at the University Level
Working Thesis: Though academic coaching is new to the college arena and has some challenges, its strengths can be very beneficial in helping first-year students transition to their new academic demands.

I. The Need for Academic Coaching at the College Level
    a. The transition from high school to college can be a very challenging experience.
        i. Students often bring unhealthy habits that were not detrimental to student success from high school to college.
            1. Lack of study habits
            2. Lack of attendance
            3. Poor time management
        ii. Independent learning is a new expectation for freshman students.
            1. No more reward systems
            2. First time in unstructured setting
                a. No structure created by parents and teachers
    b. Academic coaching can be useful in the college setting to help students transition from high school.
        i. Academic coaching in the college setting has been designed to help students focus on strengths, goals, study skills, engagement, academic planning and performance.
            1. Academic coaching builds on strengths.
            2. Goal setting is critical to help students navigate their success.
            3. The academic coach works with the student to acquire effective study strategies.

4. Student engagement is essential for retention and interest.
5. Academic planning is needed to explore student motivation, academic history and goals.
   c. There is not an agreed upon model that streamlines the academic coaching process.
      i. Academic coaching for students is fairly new with limited studies.
      ii. There is a need to study the existing academic coaching models in the college setting.

II. Coaching defined by the literature
   a. Coaching has been defined as students and coaches working collaboratively to be strategic in establishing and achieving their academic goals.
   b. Coaching is defined as one-on-one interaction with a student focusing on strengths, goals, study skills and engagement.
   c. Students in Parker's study defined coaching as a personalized, self-directed service that promotes self-determination.
   d. Another student defined coaching as a personalized service that encourages thoughtful risk-taking through experimentation with new strategies.
   e. Other students defined coaching as a nonjudgmental model in which they felt free to try out new organizational or academic techniques.
   f. The similarities and differences in coaching definitions.
   g. Some articles expressed how coaching differs from therapy.

III. Coaching models
   a. Robinson's coaching model focuses on three main steps: self-assessment, reflection and goal setting.
   b. For a number of studies, the approach is based on an inquiry model built on the belief that students are able to generate their own agenda and strategies when effectively engaged in reflective thinking.

    i. *In Parker's study, coaches focus on using questioning techniques to elicit goals, plans and strategies from the students.*

    ii. *In Swartz's study, questioning is used to help clients gain awareness of how they are changing their behavior.*

  c. *The main elements of the coaching model in Swartz's study include monitoring weekly progress, rewards, and consequences.*

  d. *All use some form of pre and post assessment along with some form of education.*

IV. Strengths of the coaching models used in these studies

  a. *The strengths highlighted in the case study included their usefulness in the early sessions to identify coping techniques to find out what clients have done well and to give them some positive feedback. This was believed to help with initial motivation and the belief that they can make changes.*

  b. *Instituting consequences for missed coaching time helped endure their commitment.*

  c. *Having participants learn to monitor their own behavior was one of the desired outcomes of the coaching process.*

  d. *Robinson's study concluded that the coaching model used in the study brought coaches and students together to create tangible plans that ultimately help students reach their academic and engagement goals.*

V. Challenges of coaching used in these studies

  a. *Psychoeducation would have been more effective if done in small segments at a time and handouts or written reminders are used.*

  b. *Prospective researcher may want to consider developing an objective measure that assesses change in participants without relying on self-reports.*

  c. *There are threats to validity in the study that should have been carefully evaluated. These threats include timing of the intervention (relative to the semester grades and exams), use of a non-standardized outcome measure and short baseline length.*

Journal

While most of the prewriting techniques described in this section occur once research has been completed, journaling is one technique that can be utilized while still gathering and reading scholarship. When journaling, writers informally note their thoughts about a subject in a book dedicated to housing ideas. Once all of the research has been completed on a subject, writers review their journal and can organize their thoughts more formally or begin the next stage of the writing process based on the information in the journal. Due to the amount of journal notes compiled based upon a topic, an example of journaling is not provided in this short section.

Using any of the prewriting techniques described in this chapter helps graduate scholars to sift through their thoughts about a subject and its affiliated research. Graduate students can experiment with various techniques if they do not have a current method of organizing ideas that works for them. One method of prewriting can be used or several can be applied at different stages of the information gathering and organizing process. The goal for graduate scholars is to pinpoint a prewriting technique or techniques that fit their preferred way of processing information, but graduate students should remain open to trying different prewriting strategies for various genres of writing. Regardless of the specific prewriting technique used, each one is designed to allow scholars to sequence their ideas, formulate their position on a topic and identify sub-points to support their position.

As evidenced through the information described in this chapter, strategic decision making is an enormous aspect of the prewriting stage. Thinking critically about and answering specific questions lead writers to clear ideas about a subject. The prewriting stage of the writing process equips writers with a blueprint for their academic writing. Armed with a sense of their document's purpose, audience, working thesis and supporting evidence, graduate scholars have a writing plan that they can execute during stage two of the writing process.

CHAPTER | 4

Draft Properly

The second stage of the writing process is producing a complete draft. Though writing occurs in the first stage, the initial draft is where ideas are expressed in sentence form, from paragraph to paragraph and section to section. With the audience and purpose pinpointed, a working thesis composed, main supporting points identified and a sense of the order in which to present ideas determined, a graduate scholar is ready to produce a full document. The draft should be composed according to the three components of document organization: introduction, body and conclusion.

Stage Two: Draft

Regardless of their length, all drafts should have a full introduction that includes a working thesis, body paragraphs that develop ideas fully with sufficient support and a conclusion that reiterates the main idea as well as brings closure to the work. Writing has a formulaic structure to it; the oft-used writing prescription by those within English circles to help those outside of the discipline apply the proper writing formula is based on Aristotle's early description of rhetoric. Today, the same formula is often taught in public speaking classes; it is, "Tell them (the audience) what you're going to tell them, then tell them, and finally, tell them what you told them" (Baldoni). No matter the type of scholarly writing, graduate scholars need to provide a general overview of their ideas in the introduction, express the details of their ideas in the body of the document and bring closure to their ideas in the conclusion.

Master the Body Paragraph

By far, the body of the draft, which is sandwiched between the introduction and conclusion, represents the bulk of writing. Though the introduction comes first, it is not always drafted first. Much more attention should be given to the body, also called the middle section, of a draft because it houses the detailed contents of a document. Therefore, the middle portion, or body, of a draft is described first in this chapter.

The middle section includes one body paragraph after another. The body paragraph represents the fundamental unit of writing organization; in essence, it is a micro-level model of any written document. By learning to properly compose body paragraphs, graduate scholars can master writing organization at a larger level. When drafting, writers need to know the four types of sentences that comprise the body paragraph. Composing a strong draft requires an understanding of each sentence type and the relationship between each of them.

Formulate a Topic Sentence

The topic sentence captures the main idea of a body paragraph and is usually the first sentence of a paragraph; all body paragraphs need one central idea. The reason to start a new body paragraph is either a new main idea is introduced or a shift in the central idea of the current paragraph occurs. Since every body paragraph has one main idea, all the other sentences in the paragraph work to explain the one central idea stated, a structure which creates paragraph focus and unity.

Provide Supporting Sentences

Supporting sentences validate the topic sentence; they are the specific sub-points that undergird the main idea expressed in the topic sentence. While the topic sentence is a broad statement, supporting sentences provide targeted explanations of the topic sentence. The number of supporting sentences in a body paragraph depends on the number of sub-points a writer has to fully explain the main idea of the paragraph.

Add Detailing Sentences

Detailing sentences give concrete examples, research and other types of evidence for the supporting sentences. As their name indicates, detailing sentences are the most descriptive of all of the sentences in a body paragraph. The number of detailing sentences in a body paragraph varies;

however, each supporting sentence should have at least one detailing sentence. Though detailing sentences specifically clarify supporting sentences, they indirectly relate to the topic sentence. The relationship between the three types of sentences is simple; each supporting sentence validates the topic sentence directly while each detailing sentence directly authenticates a supporting sentence, yet all three sentences are connected, either directly or indirectly.

Compose a Concluding Sentence

The concluding sentence brings closure to the paragraph and usually is the last sentence of a body paragraph. The central idea of the paragraph should be reiterated in the concluding sentence. Though the topic sentence should not be written verbatim in the concluding sentence, the main idea expressed in the topic sentence needs to be reinforced in the concluding sentence. The concluding sentence also can function as a transition sentence to create a smooth flow from the main idea of the current body paragraph to the main idea of the next body paragraph. However, a separate transition sentence should follow the concluding sentence.

Sample Body Paragraph

When drafting, graduate scholars should follow the simple formula of expressing one main idea per body paragraph through a topic sentence; the topic sentence is developed with supporting and detailing sentences. The paragraph ends with a concluding sentence or a transitional sentence after the concluding sentence (transitions are explained fully in the next chapter).

The paragraph below, which comes from an actual dissertation, illustrates how each sentence of a body paragraph works together to support the central idea expressed in the topic sentence. Each sentence is labeled as either a topic, supporting, detailing or concluding sentence; the label is in parentheses at the end of the sentence; following the label is an explanation of the function of that sentence in the body paragraph. Citations have been removed from the paragraph in order to include sentence type and description.

Body Paragraph from a Dissertation

Controversy and irony surround the historical reality of American slavery and its contributions to Southern history and society (***topic sentence***: *captures the main idea of the "controversies and ironies of slavery" as well as what slavery contributed to "Southern history and society," a broad subject that needs support*). One controversy about slavery exists among historians who attempt to describe the relationship between slavery and the Civil War (***supporting sentence 1***: *supports the topic sentence by focusing on a particular controversy about slavery*). Some historians contend that slavery was the direct cause of the Civil War (***detailing sentence***: *lends support to the first supporting sentence about controversy by providing a specific example of what a group of historians assert*). Others believe slavery created the larger issue of state rights, which prompted the war (***detailing sentence***: *further explains the controversy stated in the first supporting sentence by detailing differing beliefs of a second group of historians*).

Still others believe that economics, not slavery, was the driving force of the historic war dividing the North and South (*detailing sentence: gives another example of the controversy expressed in the first supporting sentence by explaining a focus of a third group of historians*). Whether slavery directly or indirectly caused the Civil War, the irony of its existence is that its reputation as one of the South's most unusual cultural institutions has had a lasting impact on the culture of the South (*supporting sentence 2: supports the topic sentence by identifying a specific irony of slavery in relation to its impact on Southern society*). Slavery, though an embarrassment to contemporary society, has defined Southern history, shaped Southern society and distinguished Southern values, politics and attitudes about race relations from Northern ones (*detailing sentence: provides specific examples of the irony of slavery*). The controversies and ironies about slavery have made it the topic of choice for countless historians, sociologists, filmmakers, psychologists, authors and scholars; however, this study explores another cultural institution originating in early Southern history that, like slavery, has proven to be a powerful, enduring force in Southern society (*concluding sentence: brings closure to the body paragraph by reiterating the main idea about slavery stated in the topic sentence while also transitioning to the central idea of the next paragraph*).

As the paragraph above illuminates, the key objective for graduate scholars when drafting body paragraphs is to construct each sentence so that it furthers the central idea stated in the topic sentence. Graduate scholars should replicate this body paragraph structure in every paragraph in the middle section of a scholarly document.

Incorporate and Cite Research Properly

Research, or various forms of proven evidence, is the hallmark of scholarly writing. Research gives credence to and validates the intellectual rigor of information presented in a scholar's work. Though the central ideas written in an academic document should be original, they need to be informed by established scholarship within the discourse community.

Because scholarly writing is evidence based, it needs to be fully supported with academically sound examples, studies, theories and other forms of research that have been through a process to validate the accuracy and scholarly merit of the information. Many of the supporting and detailing sentences of a body paragraph for scholarly documents contain specific pieces of evidence; therefore, graduate scholars must become proficient in writing about research when drafting.

Graduate scholars are expected to demonstrate academic authority and credibility by borrowing from the work of established scholars, researchers and practitioners. The borrowed research of others can occur through summarizing, paraphrasing or quoting directly. However, graduate scholars always must give credit to the appropriate authors for incorporating any of their concepts, words, research or ideas. Credit is given through an abbreviated in-text citation and an end-of-document full citation so that readers know the information, whether summarized, paraphrased or quoted directly, is not the author's and can locate the sources for themselves if they so choose. If information is not properly cited, then a graduate scholar is guilty of plagiarizing.

Graduate scholars are not only expected to cite information properly when including research, but also know the distinct reasons for summarizing, paraphrasing and quoting directly. Part of being a skilled writer is knowing how to weave evidence seamlessly into one's ideas. Information should be included verbatim, also known as directly quoting, when the original word choice is powerful and needs to be captured word for word. Additionally, factual information, like statistics, should be quoted directly. In addition to knowing when to quote directly, graduate scholars need to know how to quote directly; direct quotes need to be properly introduced rather than included as stand-alone sentences.

Paraphrases and summaries are both written in a graduate scholar's words, but they serve different purposes. Paraphrasing should be used when writers want to include information but prefer to use their own words. Paraphrasing is effective for making heavy jargon, complex ideas and other potentially confusing aspects of research more accessible to the audience; paraphrases are typically about the same length as the original content, so paraphrasing is not effective for lengthy pieces of information. Summarizing, on the other hand, condenses lengthy pieces of information; therefore, it is effective for sharing full studies, case studies, articles and other research. The same critical reading and critical thinking skills required to write an annotation are needed to properly summarize a source because only the most salient points should be included.

When writers develop a system for incorporating research conducted by others, they are able to produce a complete draft with all borrowed information identified. A key strategy for incorporating research when drafting, whether the research has been completed or is still being conducted, is deciding how to mark the following on the draft: ideas, language and information that originate in research sources. The borrowed information simply needs to be noted, not cited, when drafting.

For example, graduate scholars may not always remember or have immediate access to a source while drafting; however, they know that information they are writing did not originate with them. Instead of ceasing to write, a scholar can simply place the word "cite" in parentheses after the borrowed information and continue drafting. It is not imperative to include all in-text citations in a draft; in fact, it is counterproductive to interrupt a writing flow to locate a source. Instead, graduate scholars can bold, italicize, highlight or in some other way note the research they know is borrowed and then return to provide the complete information only after a full draft is completed.

When drafting, graduate scholars must be mindful to either summarize, paraphrase or directly quote all outside scholarship. The formatting of in-text and end of work citations is discussed more in a later chapter, when an explanation of the final stages of the writing process is provided.

Graduate Student Advice on Research

- *Catalogue assigned readings properly.*
- *Have solid background knowledge and look for topics that interest you.*
- *Read up on the research process.*
- *Plan out your research proposal as soon as you can.*
- *Use citation manager resources and software.*
- *Have ideas about what you want to do for your research at the beginning of the program.*
- *Read as much as possible in order to define research interests early on.*
- *Know expectations of research contributions, including basic knowledge and foundations required for research.*
- *Use Mandalay, Atlas TI or endnote to organize research.*
- *Start early on the research.*
- *Use plagiarism software, like TurnItIn, to your advantage when you're not sure if you have cited information properly.*
- *Never stop reading! Not only does it help you to develop your research plan but it also helps you to learn writing styles in your field.*

Write Introduction and Conclusion Paragraphs

Many writers draft the introductory and concluding paragraphs after completing the body paragraphs. Such decisions reflect personal preference. The introduction and conclusion paragraphs of a document typically do not follow the same structure as body paragraphs. For many academic disciplines, these two paragraphs lend themselves to more creativity, experimentation and innovation. Also, introduction and conclusion paragraphs usually are not as lengthy as body paragraphs.

The introduction and conclusion paragraphs have unique functions in a document. The introduction provides an overview of the topic, includes background information in certain academic documents, states the thesis and, for many disciplines, engages the reader in the subject in an interesting way. While a full introduction is not required for a writer to begin drafting the body of a document, a working thesis is needed to ensure each body paragraph supports the central idea of the entire work. The conclusion brings closure to the document while reiterating the central position of the document; depending on the type of project, the conclusion can include recommendations, calls-to-action, and/or concrete solutions.

The chart below lists some common methods of engaging a reader in an introduction and bringing closure to a document; again, heed disciplinary norms when it comes to these more creatively inclined paragraphs.

Strategies for gaining interest for a topic in an introduction	Strategies for bringing closure in a conclusion
• Ask a probing question • Tell an engaging story • Create a hypothetical situation • Present the outcome first	• Pose areas for further research • Present recommendations • Call reader to action • Provide a solution

Remember the Goal of Drafting

Too often, graduate scholars are guilty of making their academic writing an event rather than a process. When they make writing an event, students mistakenly expect to write a perfect draft and can become fixated on one small aspect of the document, such as thinking of an exact word they would like to use, repeatedly rewriting one sentence or pondering proper punctuation. This approach to drafting is time-consuming, stressful and counterproductive; it interrupts the creative flow of translating thoughts in the mind to words on paper or computer.

Knowing the goal of drafting can prevent writing anxiety during this stage of the process. Wynne, Guo and Wang designed a study to help dissertating graduate students overcome anxiety while writing. They first distinguished between writing apprehension, writing anxiety and writer's block. The scholars borrowed Bloom's definition of writing anxiety to note that those who experience it are "intellectually capable" of writing but have developed "one or a combination of feelings, beliefs, or behaviors" that interfere with the ability to "start, work on or finish a given writing task" (368). The scholars noted that context often contributes to writing anxiety. Contextual realities, such as negative family situations or poor health conditions, and negative emotions, such as the fear of failure, unrealistic expectations and the pressure to perform perfectly, often cause writing anxiety (Ondrusek 182; Wynne, Guo and Wang 371).

Graduate scholars must remember that the goal of an initial draft is to get all ideas on paper in an organized way, not a perfect way (Hacker 21). It is nearly impossible to produce a polished scholarly document with a clear argument that is well-developed and supported in one draft. Academic writing requires several iterations, so graduate scholars should allocate sufficient time to revisit an initial draft in order to improve it. When graduate scholars plan to produce multiple versions of a document, they remove the unrealistic self-imposed pressure to write a perfect document the first time.

The draft is the opportunity to ensure that all ideas have been expressed in writing from introduction to conclusion; however, writers intend to reevaluate the initial draft in order to polish and perfect it.

CHAPTER | 5

Understand All Editing is Not the Same

Both of the last two stages of the writing process are commonly referred to as editing. However, editing has two categories, which are developmental editing and line editing. Revision is synonymous with the first type, developmental editing, and is the third stage of the writing process. The goal of revision is to strengthen the expression, organization and flow of ideas in a document.

Stage Three: Revise

The purpose of revising is to re-examine (i.e., "re-see" or "re-envision") the ideas and their organization to make them clearer, stronger and more convincing. Revising involves searching for and correcting problems with content, not grammar, as well as determining ways to improve the articulation of ideas. Ideally, some amount of time should elapse between drafting and revising a document in order for the writer to gain a fresh perspective of the work (Hacker 27). The length of time between the second and third stages of the writing process is not significant; writers can wait hours, days or weeks to revise

69

a document, as long as they do not immediately attempt to revise a draft they have just completed.

Revision is critical for scholarly writing for multiple reasons. For one, scholars spend days, weeks and months researching and reading information. As a result, they become very knowledgeable concerning their research topics and academic disciplines. Such intimacy with scholarship can lead writers to unintentionally omit vital information, fail to clarify concepts and overlook obvious assumptions when drafting. Secondly, research at the graduate level is often complicated, complex and multi-layered, causing a scholar's understanding of a subject to constantly shift, deepen and evolve. Therefore, a scholar's perspective, evidence and support can change drastically and frequently between the prewriting, drafting and revising stages.

To revise effectively, graduate scholars want to imagine themselves as their intended audience who is reading the document for the very first time (Hacker 28). This mental exercise creates intellectual distance from the writing. With a fresh perspective, a scholar is prepared to assess the clarity of the writing, at the word level, phrase level, sentence level, paragraph level and section level.

Answer Specific Questions When Revising

When revising a document, writers address specific questions. The first question to consider is, "What information needs to be added to the current work to fully clarify the ideas contained within it?" Usually, additional information is needed to support ideas completely. Some content to add during the revision stage in order to illuminate ideas is background information, theoretical underpinnings, definitions and/or research.

A second question to ask when revising is, "What information should be removed because it is redundant?" Repetition is beneficial as a coherence strategy; however, a writer should strategically, not unnecessarily, repeat information. When revising a draft, writers should eliminate excessive discussion of topics and any restatements of ideas; some people tend to express the same thought several different ways to make their point. While this strategy is valued when speaking, it is not reflective of strong writing. Additionally, scholars sometimes become emotionally attached to information; therefore, they include ideas that they like but that are not connected to the central tenets of their work. When revising, writers should remove all occurrences of redundancy.

The third question to pose during the revision stage is, "What information needs to be shifted to achieve a better flow?" Similar ideas should be situated within the same paragraph or section. At times, writers begin discussing one point, shift to a different point, then return to the first point somewhere later in a document. Yet, ideas need to be fully developed when they are introduced rather than scattered periodically between other ideas or points. As discussed in the drafting chapter, every sentence in a body paragraph should support the topic sentence. When information contained within a paragraph or section does not support the topic sentence or focus of that section, it needs to be moved to the paragraph or section where the subject is discussed or deleted.

The final question to answer when revising is, "What information should be replaced because the current information is not suitable?" Often, language use does not fit the academic context of the work. When revising, graduate scholars should replace overused, misused or ineffective use of jargon, informal language, colloquialisms and other words that do not mirror the academic nature of the document. Sometimes, the language is fine, yet the evidence is weak, mismatched or insufficient. When revising, graduate scholars need to examine whether the scholarship and language used truly match the ideas presented.

Improve Coherence

Since academic writing involves analyzing and synthesizing information from multiple sources, unifying the scholarship of others with one's original thoughts can pose significant challenges during the drafting stage when a writer's focus is getting all his or her ideas on paper. The revision stage of the writing process allows writers to enhance the coherence of a document.

Coherence refers to the presentation of ideas in a logical, unified manner and is a characteristic of high quality writing. Coherence is best achieved by constantly thinking of the connection between and flow of ideas, so it is not limited to one stage of the writing process. When researching, graduate scholars need to consider how various pieces of scholarship are connected. When arranging ideas and research, graduate scholars need to organize information based on the relationships they perceive and want to explore between established scholarship and their ideas. When drafting, graduate scholars need to decide where to start and where to end so that a reader can follow their ideas easily. So, coherence within a document is the result of constant thought and effort throughout every stage of the writing process.

Since coherence is perfected during the revision stage, it is included in this chapter. When revising, writers assess ways to improve their draft so that the ideas contained within it are organized in the most logical, unified way. Thus, the questions outlined earlier (what to add; what to remove; what to shift; what to replace) are asked with the goal of creating a unified document that flows well from one section to the next.

Learn Useful Coherence Devices

To improve their scholarly writing, graduate scholars should familiarize themselves with language tools designed to connect words in a smooth, understandable way from the beginning to the end of a document. These language tools are known as coherence devices, and some of the most beneficial ones are explained below.

Incorporate Transitional Words, Phrases and Sentences

Most graduate scholars are familiar with transitions and their function of shifting a reader smoothly from one point to another. However, some graduate scholars do not realize that transitions occur at the phrase, sentence and section level in scholarly writing, not just the word level. When a writer moves from point to point, a transition provides the reader with a signal, much like traffic signs direct drivers on the road. Transitions also clarify relationships between ideas by making explicit to a reader what is evident to the writer but not always stated. For example, a transition might alert a reader to the similarities or differences between two ideas or show the chronological order of concepts described in a section.

The appendix has a comprehensive list of commonly used transitional words and phrases as well as the relationships they illustrate. However, it is important for graduate scholars to see transitional elements in a scholarly writing context. The sentences below, which are taken from graduate level work, demonstrate how transitional words move a reader from one idea to the next as well as illuminate relationships between concepts expressed in writing. The transitional elements are bolded while the role of the transition is explained in parentheses.

Traditional Words in a Graduate Level Document

> Religion is defined as a structured system of traditions, beliefs, and symbols designed to support closeness to the transcendent or sacred, such as God or higher truth. *Moreover, (a transition word indicating what follows is an additional definition of the word that was provided already)* religion is conceptualized as facilitating an understanding of one's responsibility to others while residing in a community together (Koenig, McCullough, & Larson, 2001). *In contrast, (a transitional phrase that signals the following definition is vastly different from the definition provided in the previous sentences)* spirituality is defined as an individual quest for understanding answers to questions, such as a life's meaning and connection to the sacred (i.e., God).

Understand Parallel Constructions

Also known as parallelism, parallel construction is using the same pattern and sentence structure to show that the ideas presented carry the same level of importance. Like transitions, parallelism can be applied at the word, phrase, clause or sentence level.

The goal of parallelism is to balance similar ideas, showing the reader their equality and causing ideas to be more readily understood. Most graduate scholars know how to create parallel constructions when listing information at the word level to show their equality, such as in the following example which has parallel words italicized, "The research used *surveys*, *questionnaires* and *interviews* to gather data on student alcohol consumption."

Also, graduate scholars typically are familiar with parallelism at the phrase level, such as in the following sentence, "Based on several of Johnson's observations, members of the governing officials initiated numerous social and cultural projects to *manage the city's sanitary conditions, educate the population, organize projects to improve existing public spaces* and *create new spaces for public recreation*." Each of the italicized phrases begins with a verb and ends with a noun; these parallel constructions demonstrate that each of these activities carries equal value.

However, many graduate scholars are not as aware of creating parallelism at the sentence level. Some of the sentences included above to illustrate transitional words can be studied for parallelism. Looking at the sentences below, which have been modified slightly, note that the first sentence and the third sentence are written in a parallel way to show that the definitions for "religion" and "spirituality" have equal weight. The parallel sentences are bolded and italicized; in parentheses after the sentence is an explanation of the parallel construction.

Parallelism at the Sentence Level in a Graduate Level Document

> *First, religion is defined as a structured system of traditions, beliefs, and symbols designed to support closeness to the transcendent or sacred, such as God or higher truth (begins with a transition word, has a term that is defined and uses the word order "is defined as" to explain it).* Moreover, religion is conceptualized as facilitating an understanding of one's responsibility to others while residing in a community together (Koenig, McCullough, & Larson, 2001). *Secondly, spirituality is defined as an individual quest for understanding answers to questions, such as a life's meaning and connection to the sacred (begins with a transition word, has a term that is defined and uses the word order "is defined as" to explain it).*

Repeat Key Terms

Repetition is not normally embraced positively in scholarly writing; however, to repeat key terms is essential for ensuring that central ideas remain before the reader. The words that represent the thrust of the ideas to be explored in a document are known as key terms. Graduate scholars should strategically repeat key terms to create unity throughout a document. One way to ensure that strategic repetition does not become redundant is to replace key terms with synonyms and pronouns for the key terms.

Consider the following sentence that presents the subject of a research article, with the key terms bolded: "Several **educational researchers** promote **non-**

traditional approaches to education as viable options for **improving** test **scores**." Once key terms are pinpointed, synonyms for them should be identified and used interchangeably throughout the document. The italicized synonyms or pronouns in parentheses after the key terms in the sentence below serve as excellent substitutes: "Several **educational researchers** (*specific names of researchers or the pronoun "they" can be used interchangeably*) promote **non-traditional** (*"unconventional" and "alternative" can be used interchangeably*) **approaches** (*"methods," "techniques" and "they" can be used interchangeably*) to education as viable options for **improving** (*"increasing" and "strengthening" can be used interchangeably*) test **scores** (*"results," "marks" and "they" can be used interchangeably*)." Once identified, at least one of the key terms, its synonym or pronoun should be used in each sentence of the document to create coherence. When key terms permeate a document through strategic repetition, writers are forced to remain focused on unifying main ideas from the introduction to the conclusion.

Create a Reading Rhythm

Paragraph proportionality also creates unity in a document. A consistent paragraph length creates a rhythm, flow and connectedness between ideas for readers. While graduate scholars should utilize sentence variety in their writing, they should not move from short, choppy body paragraphs to large, chunky body paragraphs. Experienced writers establish a sentence quantity range for their body paragraphs and commit to composing body paragraphs that stay within the established range, a technique that creates a reading rhythm from page to page.

When learning to revise effectively, graduate scholars may need to scrutinize a document much more than they would like to in order to produce a coherent, logical scholarly work. While the number of revisions most likely will decrease with experience, graduate scholars should realize that even experienced writers conduct multiple revisions; repeated revision is simply part of the process of creating sound scholarly writing.

In fact, revision varies from document to document; some documents take one or two revisions while others require dozens of revision, no matter how experienced the writer may be. Often, external deadlines dictate the number of revisions that realistically can be conducted. However, only after graduate scholars are satisfied with the organization, coherence and clarity of ideas expressed in a document should they move to the final stage of the writing process.

Stage Four: Proofread

Proofreading, or line/copy editing, is the final step of the writing process. Proofreading is finding and correcting problems with grammar, stylistic issues like passive voice, punctuation and other language mechanics. Once scholars are comfortable with the content of a document, they should proofread it.

Avoid Blending the Two Types of Editing

As emphasized at the beginning of this chapter, content editing focuses on macro level issues of idea flow, coherence and organization while line editing corrects micro level issues of spelling, grammar and punctuation. Though writers should correct blatant mechanical problems, like misspelled words or punctuation errors, when revising, they should not allow their focus to become grammar until the final stage of the writing process.

The acts of improving larger issues of content and correcting smaller issues of mechanics require different types of concentration. When writers shift their focus from developmental editing to line editing while revising, they often lose sight of the big picture and can no longer identify organizational problems. The result of this shift is usually a grammatically correct document that lacks clarity, unity and continuity of ideas. Great expertise is needed to conduct content and line editing simultaneously.

Therefore, graduate scholars should resist the urge to combine revising and proofreading into one step. Though doing so may save time and effort, it often does not produce the best scholarly writing. Additionally, by combining proofreading and revising, writers can waste valuable time correcting parts of the document that may not even survive the revision stage. Recall that one of the questions to answer when revising is, "What information needs to be eliminated?" Words, sentences, paragraphs and sometimes entire sections of a document are removed during the revision stage, so graduate scholars should proofread only after revision has been completed.

Make the Right Assumption

Since most writers spend a significant amount of time revising a document before proofreading it, they mistakenly believe their document is error free. However, when writers make the opposite assumption - that grammar errors are present in a document, regardless of how many times it has been reviewed by themselves or others - they alertly search for and locate remaining errors.

Utilize Proofreading Techniques

Several proofreading strategies have been documented to assist writers in overcoming the familiarity they have with their documents. One approach is to read the document out loud, which forces the writer to hear the words written on the page rather than the words he or she intended to write (Hacker 30-31). Another effective proofreading technique is reading the document from the last page to the first page (Hacker 30-31). This approach disrupts the writer's knowledge of the document's organization, thus allowing the writer to focus on grammar and revealing overlooked errors from previous readings of the work.

For graduate scholars who are not confident in their knowledge of English language rules, ample grammar resources are available. Writing centers, colleagues with an expert command of the English language and professional editors are useful for polishing scholarly works. Additionally, a plethora of handbooks, websites, podcasts and other educational resources exist for improving English language mechanics.

Every person has a distinct writing style and makes consistent errors when writing. A writing expert can pinpoint graduate scholars' problematic areas of grammar as well as direct them to the proper resources for helping them to become proficient self-reviewers. Regardless of how it is accomplished, proofreading allows graduate scholars to grammatically perfect their writing, which is judged for its accurate use of language as well as the quality of its content.

Differentiate between Style and Grammar

Another important writing element graduate scholars should consider when proofreading is style, which is distinct from grammar. Grammar dictates whether writing is correct or incorrect whereas style also includes whether writing is appropriate or inappropriate for a particular context, audience or discipline. Therefore, something that is grammatically correct for all disciplines can be stylistically correct in one field while stylistically incorrect in a different one. Style in this context does not refer to a writing style but references non-grammar issues that have guidelines to dictate whether they are correct.

Many graduate scholars are much more confident about grammar rules than stylistic norms. For example, graduate scholars know the grammar rule governing subject-verb agreement; it states that verbs must agree with their subject in number, so if a singular verb is used with a plural subject, they recognize that it is incorrect. However, stylistic guidelines are more ambiguous. One prominent and sometimes perplexing area of style that should be examined when proofreading is the use of voice.

In the English language, sentences are written in either active voice or passive voice. A sentence written in active voice has the subject of the sentence written before the verb; however, a sentence written in passive voice has the verb written before the subject. The selection of which voice to use impacts sentence structure, sentence subject and sentence length. The two sentences below express the same idea; however, one is written in passive voice while the other is written in active voice.

Passive Voice	The ground-breaking research was conducted by several prominent scholars in the field of medicine.
Active Voice	Several prominent scholars in the field of medicine conducted the ground-breaking research.

Depending on the discipline of a scholar, he or she would need, during the proofreading stage, to rewrite the sentence to change it from passive to active voice. Grammatically, nothing is wrong with writing in passive voice. However, it is greatly discouraged in the Social Sciences and Humanities, unless used for a particular purpose. Within these disciplines, writing in passive voice should be a conscious choice a writer can defend rather than a habit that reflects a rudimentary understanding of style. For example, passive voice permeates this book to emphasize actions rather than subjects. In many STEM areas, specifically Engineering, writing in passive voice is completely acceptable and rather commonplace. When scholars in these fields use passive voice, it is not viewed as a haphazard, lethargic use of language.

Another area of style that can cause confusion is the use of the final comma before the "and" when listing three or more words or phrases. Throughout this guide, a final comma is not used before "and;" however, some style guides dictate that a final comma should be used before "and" when listing. Adding or omitting a final comma before the "and" is grammatically correct as long as the use is consistent throughout a document. Yet, certain disciplines may consider one of the uses stylistically incorrect. Graduate scholars are responsible for knowing and consistently applying stylistic rules that align with their disciplinary conventions.

Access Academic Resources to Master Style

Though stylistic areas of writing can be confusing, resources exist to eliminate stylistic uncertainty. In fact, graduate scholars must master nuanced issues of style within a specific academic arena in order to produce polished scholarly works. Disciplinary writing style guides are indispensable for learning what is stylistically acceptable, and various fields have different guides. For example, scholars in education use the American Psychological Association (APA) style manual while those in English and Foreign Languages use the Modern Language Association (MLA).

Style manuals delineate citation guidelines, formatting issues and stylistic writing norms. All graduate scholars need a personal copy, whether print or electronic, of the style manual that governs their discipline. Furthermore, graduate scholars should reference these guides whenever they have disciplinary writing questions and especially when proofreading to ensure their documents are stylistically correct, formatted correctly and properly cited. Style manuals explain and provide examples of how to cite any type of research source imaginable, from personal interviews to anthologies. The manuals also include examples of scholarly works so that graduate scholars can see the principles applied in an academic writing context.

In-text and end-of-document citations were discussed in the drafting chapter. All information from research should be cited during the revision stage. Since research can extend into the revision stage, all citation and formatting issues should be finalized during the proofreading stage. Several reputable software programs store, organize, manage and format references; campus libraries typically host workshops to instruct graduate scholars in the use of the electronic citation resources to which the university subscribes; additionally, librarians are excellent teachers of citation management software. Though citation programs, much like spell check, eliminate stress and save time, they can overlook certain errors. Therefore, the use of electronic sources should always be accompanied with the knowledge of how to properly utilize a disciplinary style manual to verify rules. While style is more fluid than grammar, correcting errors in both areas should be the focus of the final stage of the writing process.

Personalize the Writing Process

The four stages of the writing process should serve as a foundation for graduate students to create personal writing rituals that suit their preferences. Pinpointing locations, times of day, spaces, environments and conditions that are most conducive to productive writing can contribute to graduate scholars developing a personalized writing process that facilitates effective prewriting, drafting, revising and proofreading. For instance, some people need absolute silence to draft while others are stimulated by music to release all of the ideas out of their head. Or, a person who usually needs a clutter free environment to revise may be able to proofread in a disorganized work area.

One activity to consider integrating into a personal writing process is peer revision. Scholarly writing is a peer-reviewed genre, so graduate scholars must become comfortable releasing their writing to outside critique. Incorporating peer revision into a personal writing process can facilitate graduate students' openness to outside critique. Some people are strong content reviewers while others know English language rules extremely well. Identifying colleagues who proficiently give quality content and/or grammar feedback is valuable to maturing as a scholarly writer.

Employing a writing process gives graduate scholars the tools to craft sound scholarly writing as well as the knowledge to eliminate writing anxiety, procrastination and frustration. The fact remains that all graduate scholars can implement a systematic approach to writing that will improve document quality and increase personal confidence for producing scholarship that fulfills academic expectations.

Advice from Graduate Students on Writing

- *Make a habit of reading and writing daily.*
- *Stay focused and work every single day, even if it is only for 15 minutes at a time.*
- *Work a little each day.*
- *Develop a set schedule each week and have devoted writing time.*
- *Adopt a writing style early and prepare to write many drafts to avoid becoming attached to any one version.*
- *Enter candidacy with a proposal outline in mind.*
- *Have a peer group with those of the same discipline.*
- *Put things down on paper instead of trying to keep information in your head because you need to organize your thoughts.*
- *Develop the ability to write when relatively small chunks of time are available.*

CHAPTER | 6

Take Ownership of Graduate Education

As the chapters in this writing guide reveal, graduate students cannot afford to be novice, amateur learners who leave the responsibility of their education to professors, required readings and assigned classwork. As scholars in training, graduate students must take the necessary steps to become serious academic contenders within their disciplines. This final chapter describes the essence of graduate scholars whose actions naturally flow from their being. In order to effectively apply the writing strategies outlined in this guide, graduate students must "be" a number of things in order to consistently "do" the actions in this book.

Be Committed

Every graduate student can develop into a world class scholar who clearly communicates ideas in writing and orally because academic writing and speaking skills can be learned. Certain scholarly competencies may develop more quickly or more easily than others, yet they all can be understood, acquired and mastered.

Becoming a world class scholar requires a commitment to educational, personal and professional development. Old habits must be shed and new rituals embraced. Old patterns of learning must be divorced and new ways of comprehending married. Old thoughts must be relinquished and new philosophies acquired. For example, scholars in training should no longer consider professors to be gatekeepers of grades; instead, they need to view faculty members as academic trainers, role models and mentors. With this mentality, graduate scholars can recognize that faculty members perceive them more like protégés, evolving peers and potential colleagues than students.

When graduate scholars grasp the nature of advanced graduate study, they appreciate graduate school as a training center designed to provide access to valuable information, people, resources and tools. Then, they can dedicate themselves to benefitting fully from the opportunity to become burgeoning scholars who have carved a niche in their discipline based on a declared research interest, establishing themselves as the expert when a particular academic subject is mentioned.

Be Proactive

All graduate students, regardless of how strong they are as writers, can improve their writing. Many graduate students are challenged to overcome one of two negative attitudes towards writing: apathy or aversion. Typically, apathetic graduate students simply do not like to write, do not think their writing needs much improvement, do not realize what they need to learn or do not understand the importance of writing for obtaining a graduate degree.

Usually, graduate students with an aversion to writing have had traumatic, defeating experiences that generate extreme writing anxiety. Some of the insecurities, fears and nonchalance that graduate students have regarding writing are completely understandable considering their past writing experiences. However, too many graduate students mistakenly allow their writing history to prevent them from choosing to refine their writing until they are forced to do so.

More and more, graduate programs expect enrollees to publish before graduation in order to increase their competitiveness on the job market. Therefore, graduate scholars must be proactive in several ways.

Specific Ways Graduate Students can be Proactive

1. Take action to acquire the needed writing knowledge, skills and abilities to be successful.
2. Dismiss negative emotions and history about writing.
3. Overcome feelings of embarrassment, shame and inferiority by realizing you are among many others who must overcome the same writing challenges, fears and insecurities.
4. Stay motivated to invest the required effort to develop their writing.

Be Professional

A professional, unlike an amateur, is an expert in the work that he or she does. The ability to earn a living based on the level of knowledge, precision and skill developed distinguishes professionals from amateurs. Amateurs typically possess an interest, passion or affinity for a particular activity yet are unwilling to invest what is necessary to become recognized professionals.

All professionals, whether in the educational, athletic or business arena, share certain qualities; being intentional is one of their most critical traits. To obtain a successful outcome, professionals deliberately learn and apply techniques, strategies and skills that bring an expected result. Professionals willingly work hard, sacrifice and extend beyond their comfort zones to excel in their craft. Professionals diligently commit to learning systematic approaches to obtain the outcomes they desire. Likewise, graduate students must be intentional in their actions, inside and outside the classroom, if they expect to develop into scholars.

Professionals intentionally invest time and effort to acquire access to valuable information, resources and networks. Professionals seek out and surround themselves with mentors, coaches and those who have either accomplished what they strive to achieve or have proven they can teach others to obtain success. Professionals understand the value of building relationships with those who possess insider information and can share tips in addition to potential mistakes, hazards and distractions. In the academic realm, professors, advisors, program directors, committee members, university administrators and researchers are the professionals who represent a powerful pool of mentors, advocates, resource guides and coaches for graduate students.

Enrolling in graduate school is a deliberate act that must be followed by additional calculated actions because producing sound scholarship does not automatically result from attending class, reading course materials and completing course assignments. The return on the investment of time, money and energy to earn an advanced degree is only realized when graduate students commit to becoming professionals in the educational arena; they dedicate themselves to becoming professional learners, readers, thinkers and writers.

Traits of a Professional

Traits of a Professional

1. Focused	6. Persevering
2. Consistent	7. Accountable
3. Disciplined	8. Strategic
4. Willing	9. Intentional
5. Patient	10. Resourceful

The statistics regarding advanced graduate education are real: approximately half of those who start a doctoral program finish (Council of Graduate Schools). Many potential barriers can prevent graduate students from succeeding, such as being the member of an underrepresented gender, socioeconomic class, ethnic group or race in one's discipline. Other circumstances can pose a barrier to graduate school success, such as an unsupportive educational atmosphere, educational politics, family crises, faculty infighting, health problems, the lack of role models, financial struggles or the lack of writing instruction. However, each of these obstacles can be overcome. What remains insurmountable is an individual lack of personal accountability. Without a doubt, the lack of personal agency will extinguish any chance of earning an advanced graduate degree.

Advice from Graduate Students on Earning an Advanced Degree

- *Read Getting What You Came For by Robert Peters before beginning the program.*
- *You must truly want the PhD for your own reasons, and you must decide to fully embrace the experience because it will be tough and sometimes not very rewarding.*
- *Be patient! Expect to be discouraged to the point of quitting, but know you can persevere. It may be difficult and frustrating, but the experience is well worth it.*
- *Don't relax because it's a long way to get "DR."*
- *Do not lose sight of finishing the PhD.*
- *Have a goal in mind as well as a structure/framework.*
- *Don't get consumed with your faculty members' issues.*

Conclusion

This writing guide serves as a formal introduction to scholarly writing. Consider it an academic writing starter kit on the quest to deliberately produce writing that is critical, clear and coherent. Other tools will be added to graduate students' scholarly writing development tool kit, such as intimate comprehension of the literature review and research proposal, as they matriculate from coursework to comprehensive exams to thesis/dissertation. However, graduate scholars can continually utilize this guide as a resource, knowing that its value in year two will differ from its significance during semester one because of the scholarly maturation process that is inherent to graduate study. Graduate students reach different stages in their scholarly mentality, acclimation to the world of academia and cultivation of their writing.

So, welcome to the world of scholarly writing. Embrace the joys, rewards and challenges of being a critical reader, critical thinker and critical writer. You and your writing will never be the same, nor should they be!

About the Author

Vernetta K. Williams, PhD, is a writing coach, editor and speaker with a B.A. in Journalism and Mass Communication from the University of North Carolina at Chapel Hill, an M.A. in English from North Carolina Agricultural and Technical State University and a PhD in English from the University of South Florida.

Vernetta utilizes her experiences as a university educator, administrator and curriculum designer to develop scholarly writing resources for graduate students. As founder of Chrysalis Consulting LLC, Vernetta works with universities, educational funds and fellowship programs to service the writing needs of graduate students and decrease the amount of time, stress and finances associated with earning a graduate degree. "Cultivate the Writer," the signature program of Chrysalis Consulting, is designed to facilitate the academic writing development of students. Through workshops, webinars, writing clinics, writing groups and other customized writing support services, the Cultivate the Writer program helps to transform graduate students into confident scholars who can publish their research.

For information about "Cultivate the Writer" academic writing development services, visit www.cultivatethewriter.com or email drv@cultivatethewriter.com

Appendix A

Author Reflections on Her Journey from Student to Scholar

I had absolutely no idea what I signed up for when I enrolled in a doctoral program. Naively, I believed earning a PhD would be similar to earning a bachelor's degree or a little more intense than obtaining a master's degree. I was warned by a mentor that getting a PhD would be hard; however, I always had excelled academically so what was difficult to others was relatively easy for me. Consequently, I did not seriously heed my mentor's warning. When my four-year journey became five years, then six years, then seven years, I became intimately acquainted with what was hard about this unique academic rite of passage. In this final section, I reflect on my academic maturation process from the master's to the doctoral level. I hope my story encourages someone!

I began graduate study as an eager master's student in English. The English discipline has three main areas of concentration: Creative Writing, Literature and Rhetoric and Composition. I started graduate study with a general knowledge of the three major concentrations and a passionate interest in African American Literature. As an undergraduate Journalism and Mass Communication major, I entered graduate school at a disadvantage to peers who were undergraduate English majors or experienced English teachers. My success at this first step of advanced study depended on my willingness to realize what I lacked and my commitment to improving my critical thinking and critical reading skills, which in turn, developed my critical writing abilities.

Early on, I allowed my natural interests to direct my academic decision making. I focused on the sub-specialty of African American Literature within American Literature. I took courses that explored genres of literature written by African Americans during different time periods. During classes, I realized that I needed to develop an intellectual intensity for my new field of English. I quickly learned that while I shared the same passion for reading and writing as my classmates, I lacked the disciplinary knowledge of those who majored in English as undergraduates. I did not have foundational knowledge regarding my discipline and felt ignorant of so much information, including seminal texts and theories in my area of concentration.

With new motivation to catch up to my classmates, I did not read solely to comprehend, prepare for class discussions or complete an assignment. While those goals were important, I discovered what was most important was understanding the scholarly conversation, or what had been written about literary works by African Americans through the years and by whom. So, I read with a critical lens of comprehending the academic conversation as well as the viewpoints of scholars about the discipline over the years. For me, learning the conversation about African American Literature entailed becoming familiar with prominent Black novelists, poets, short story writers, critics and essay writers from various historical periods as well as traditions, literary criticism, themes and threads within this particular area of literature.

I also committed to supplementing my classroom education in this new English world with self-study. While reading assigned texts and documents for class, I paid close attention to the scholars mentioned and cited. I scoured the works cited pages of assigned journal articles for other noteworthy scholarship. I paid attention to terms, studies or theories emphasized in class, familiarizing myself with them. I kept all of my course assignments and syllabi because I was unclear about what seemed important and what was truly important, so I wanted to reference prior information as my understanding increased.

To begin building my personal library, I kept all of my graduate textbooks rather than selling them at the end of each semester, which was a common practice for me as an undergraduate. In fact, I gathered stray and old books from the English department any chance I could, a habit I continued as a doctoral student and faculty member. Over time, I became as knowledgeable and articulate about the English discipline as my peers who had majored in English as undergraduates.

My confidence increased the more I read because I could clearly articulate different schools of thought within the African American literary conversation. I began to study, understand and analyze literary theories and theorists within and beyond African American literature. I engaged in what I read by taking notes and asking questions in the margins as if speaking to the author or critic. I reread works, as needed. I examined works cited page for other documents of interest; then, I located those sources and read them. As a result, I learned key historical and contemporary scholars, seminal literary figures, important theories, significant studies and other significant aspects of the academic conversation about African American Literature. As I regularly analyzed the information I gathered, I began formulating interesting questions, thoughts and theories based on what I understood about the African American literary conversation.

Also, I established relationships beyond the classroom, which was vitally important because I was new to the university and department so I did not have existing connections with faculty, administrators or classmates. I started by asking questions regularly during class, frequenting professors' offices for individual guidance and making a regular presence in the department office and halls. As a result, I acquired a faculty mentor.

My faculty mentor invited me to become a graduate assistant in the department's Writing Center. Her invitation positioned me to conduct work that improved my understanding of the discipline. As an undergraduate, I worked solely to earn income, so I took a position in a science lab though I was a journalism major. However, my graduate level work experiences aligned with my studies and afforded me the opportunity to work alongside staff and faculty. Based upon my success tutoring students individually and learning about resources to strengthen writing in the Writing Center, I was awarded a teaching assistantship. My teaching appointment further strengthened my network of peers, colleagues and mentors within the department.

Throughout my time as a master's student, I had the opportunity to shadow my mentor, which provided invaluable insight into higher education culture, administrative decision making and faculty demands. During my first year, my mentor accepted an administrative appointment in the college. When she began traveling regularly, she asked me to teach her courses. I had to commit to extra hours preparing and late nights in my mentor's office in order to review class materials and lesson plans so that I would be comfortable teaching her classes. However, the reward was increased confidence, insider teaching techniques and the opportunity to build a strong relationship with a seasoned faculty member and newly minted College Associate Dean.

My mentor spoke to me regularly about earning my doctorate. She invited me to attend a professional conference with her so that I could glimpse the academic community beyond the classroom and local university. My mentor became so influential in my educational decision-making that the school I eventually attended to earn my doctorate was her alma mater. She described the impact of a particular faculty member on her writing and said she believed he could do the same for me. My mentor guided me through the application process and wrote a stellar recommendation letter in support of my admittance. The close relationship I developed with my mentor was a completely new experience. Prior to my master's program, I had kept a healthy distance from faculty members, viewing them in a one dimensional student-teacher fashion.

My constant presence in the departmental halls and office also facilitated a budding relationship with the Department Chair. When he learned that I intended to pursue a doctorate, he began sharing funding opportunities with me. He pulled me in his office one day and said, "I just received this fax. I'm not sure where you are considering going, but I think you should really consider this university because they are recruiting in your area." Ironically, the school was the same institution that I had applied to: my mentor's alma mater! I applied and received the doctoral fellowship, which paid my tuition, provided an annual living stipend and affiliated me with an institute on campus.

My year and a half as a master's student was a transformative experience where I learned to advocate for myself, build relationships and be more strategic with my studies. My efforts did not go unnoticed. I was nominated and selected as "Graduate Student of the Year" for the College of Arts and Sciences during my final semester of study. Most importantly, I established a mindset of assuming responsibility for my educational success, which proved useful in my doctoral program.

As an incoming doctoral student, I built upon the skills I acquired during my master's program. I committed to building a support network, engaged in academic life beyond the classroom, deepened knowledge of my discipline and secured a faculty mentor. I felt confident about the journey based upon my experiences as a master's student. Plus, I had the additional support of a built-in network as a fellow associated with a campus institute, funding that alleviated the financial pressure to work, a personal referral to a faculty member who agreed to chair my dissertation and a colleague from my master's program who decided to earn her PhD at the same university.

However, I was not prepared for the sheer volume of work and nearly quit my first semester.

With all of the skills I developed as a master's student, I still felt overwhelmed, unprepared and underqualified my first year as a doctoral student. I realized that, yet again, I needed to make immediate drastic changes if I was going to earn a PhD. Through more intentional effort, my life began to almost entirely revolve around my program of study. I began allocating more time to course readings and assignments. Excited about moving to sunny Florida, I had found some social and leisure outlets rather quickly. The reality of the intense demands of doctoral coursework forced me to spend more time with classmates and graduate students in other academic areas and less time talking to anyone not enrolled in a doctoral program.

Though I kept spiritual, physical and occasional social outlets to maintain a healthy balance, most of my out of classroom activities aligned with my program of study. With no guilt, I began declining social invites so that I could work on course assignments. I carried at least one academic book and notebook everywhere I went to maximize any time I could capture. I occupied spare minutes waiting in line or at the doctor's office with thinking about research, reading or taking notes. I began analyzing news stories, conversations, movies and other "non-academic" activities with a critical lens, thinking of a way to either apply a concept I learned in class or connect my studies with my leisure life.

In doctoral study, I focused on a new source of information to learn scholarly conversation: academic journals. Though

I was aware of journals as a master's student, I concentrated on course readings, assigned texts and the works cited pages of interesting scholarship to learn the African American literary conversation. Since I opted to take additional coursework rather than write a thesis at the end of my master's program, I did not have to conduct significant independent research and writing. Therefore, my exposure to academic journals was limited during my master's program. As a doctoral student, I more proactively examined the larger professional conversation and identified a few key journals in my discipline to review regularly.

During doctoral study, I had developed clear thoughts about the specific aspect of the African American literary conversation into which I wanted to insert myself as a scholar. So, building upon the broad exposure to the African American literary canon I gained in my master's program, I chose to specialize in two genres within Black Literature: the autobiography and historically-based novels. Since the autobiographical genre possesses certain rhetorical elements, I had to engage in a different academic arena of English (Rhetoric and Composition) in order to speak with authority about my research interest. However, I knew how to critically read and critically think in order to learn this new disciplinary discourse community.

Becoming the research assistant (RA) of a well-rounded faculty member facilitated my full acclimation to the world of academia. The position resulted from a relationship I built with the director of the institute that sponsored my fellowship. Though the faculty member was in a completely different discipline, I welcomed the opportunity because I felt isolated in my department. Her research aligned with my diverse research interests, just from a different disciplinary perspective, so I received validation, affirmation and motivation for my interests by working on her professional endeavors.

While I had great support at the institute that granted me a fellowship, I had not done due diligence in researching the faculty expertise in the English department; unfortunately, only two professors and a minute percentage of the curriculum focused on my research interests. In fact, a classmate from my master's program who shared my research interests and started the program with me left after the first year, which caused me to feel even more secluded academically. I felt most of my colleagues and professors did not value my academic pursuits.

My journey to selecting a dissertation topic that would carve out my contribution to the African American literary conversation was not linear. As I transitioned from coursework to comprehensive exams, I declared my expertise in the two genres as well as a subspecialty within one genre. I also possessed interests in the field of education due to my exposure to this field as a research assistant. Upon passing my comprehensive exams, I pursued a dissertation topic that I felt merged literature with education. However, I could not successfully convince my dissertation chair of the value of the topic.

My quest for a suitable dissertation topic continued until I returned to the tangential area of Rhetoric and Composition. This other area of English concentration opened new conceptual options to me. Upon conducting more critical thinking and critical reading, I selected theoretical frameworks that aligned with my research interests in the African American autobiography and historically based novels written by Black authors; I chose to apply broad concepts from Rhetoric and Composition to these works. I also successfully added conceptual models from cultural anthropology and social psychology that related to English based concepts. After exploring several historical periods, I decided upon the Civil Rights era based on omissions I perceived in the literature and upon which I had enough support to develop a sound argument.

Agreeing to become the research assistant for the faculty member in an outside discipline proved to be the wisest decision I made as a doctoral student because she became my mentor, advisor, encourager and role model. As a prolific grant writer, she received several national grants during my tenure with her. As a well-established scholar in her field, she regularly published and presented at professional conferences. As an academic visionary, she hosted conferences that featured national scholars and started a center on campus to house her various initiatives. As a mentor, she navigated countless students through their educational journeys. Through her professional engagement, I became intimately acquainted with the numerous roles available to a faculty member in academia; each position she fulfilled was connected to her scholarly interests.

I eventually named this faculty member my "super mentor" because of the myriad of ways she developed me educationally, professionally and personally. As her research assistant, I learned to conduct academic inquiry, search databases, collect multiple sources, critically read information, assess theory and annotate sources. I become familiar with the process of submitting research to an academic journal as well as preparing a grant application packet. I participated in gathering, preparing and organizing documents for the tenure and promotion process. I submitted abstracts for conference presentations and panels. These experiences provoked me to think more strategically about my research agenda and goals.

Eventually, my research assistant role expanded to other valuable professional opportunities. I gained experiences with grant project coordination and conference planning. I become comfortable building rapport with renowned scholars in the field, participating in committee meetings and interacting with university administrators. As my supervisor, my mentor intentionally exposed me to all facets of her work, and I willingly accepted any opportunity she presented to me. As a result, I gained a holistic perspective of academia.

Without this critical relationship and intimate access to the inner workings of higher education, I have no doubt that I would not have a PhD today. When my plan of graduating in four years did not materialize, the consistent guidance, wisdom, network and support of this faculty member sustained me during the tumultuous additional four years of study. She encouraged me through four dissertation committee chairs; she advised me through departmental politics; she challenged me to think about my research clearly; she strategized with me on effectively presenting my concerns, frustrations and needs to administrators. She referred me to resources. When I finished, she continually provided support in whatever way I requested, whether via recommendation letters, advice for a newly minted doctoral degree holder or support as a scholarly innovator.

Due to my mentor's example, I saw the value of fully aligning my personal life with my academic pursuits. I learned to merge passion with research interests. I learned how and when to advocate. I mastered many lessons, but the greatest one was thinking at a higher level by applying the critical thinking skills of scholarship to address any challenge. My relationship with my mentor during doctoral study was comparable to an apprentice being trained by a master craftsman. Each week brought access to new information, techniques or application. Without intense immersion into the life of a practicing scholar, I would not have persevered through the frustrations, disappointments or perplexities of doctoral study.

The defining lesson to take from my journey is how my education evolved throughout graduate study. When I began graduate school as a master's student in 1998, I immediately assumed responsibility to develop in areas in which I was deficient. I could no longer afford to leave my education to the assigned curriculum of the university, department or faculty members. Instead, I become an active agent in my educational success, taking ownership of learning what I needed to become an expert in my field of study. When I could only travel so far alone, my mentors navigated me through the scholarly maturation process, helping me to view some of the challenges as normal parts of the process.

My process for developing an authentic authoritative voice in African American literature deepened my knowledge of the scholarship of several academic conversations. I have a level of expertise, through years of extensive study, research and writing in the specialty areas of persuasive writing (argument) and personal narrative writing (autobiographies and memoirs) written by African Americans (specifically, historically based works written by Blacks in the South during the Civil Rights Era). I possess a depth of expertise in these areas that no one else has due to my years of critical reading, critical thinking and critical writing on these topics.

As a result of my devotion in and outside the classroom, I earned a doctoral degree in English. When it comes to literature and the English language, I am a professional. I have invested three degrees, a decade and a half of my life and more than $100,000 in becoming an expert in academic writing, the autobiography and African American Literature. I have a library of books and acquire more each year. I have been recognized and honored for my writing abilities and am able to earn a living as a professional writing coach, editor and speaker.

The doctoral degree earning process helped me commit to lifelong learning as a means of enriching who I am and what I do. My approach to everything has been forever marked by advanced graduate study. I am a scholar; therefore, I automatically engage in critical thinking, critical reading and critical writing. When I started a writing consulting company, I had to acquire new information, networks and skills. However, as a professional, my commitment to personal development caused me to seek out resources, coaches and training to become a proficient business owner. I utilized the same mentality to better service my clients that I used to improve my teaching and leadership when I was a faculty member and administrator.

As a writing coach and editor who assists people in numerous academic disciplines, I had to familiarize myself with new writing style guides, such as APA (American Psychological Association). I learned about various levels of doctoral study and their unique objectives, curricula and writing needs, including the Doctor of Nursing Practice (DNP) and Doctor of Business Administration (DBA). I studied the types of scholarly writing conducted in fields that were foreign to me before I started consulting, including Health, Engineering and Business.

However, this professional journey began when I chose to take ownership of my education as a master's student and commit to personal, educational and professional development.

Appendix B

A Guide to Writing a Research-Based Paper

Composed by Dr. Uday S. Murthy, Director, Lynn Pippenger School of Accountancy Eminent Scholar, USF Muma College of Business

Introduction
- First/second paragraphs – set up the topic; provide background; attract the reader's interest in the subject
- Second/third/fourth paragraphs – explain the problem, including why it is important and what is done in the paper to address it; clearly state the purpose and objective(s) of the paper; state the research question(s) and the basis for the expectation (theory); jargon should not be in the introduction and minimized throughout the paper
- Fourth/fifth paragraph – explain how the paper contributes to the academic body of knowledge and to practice, where applicable
- Remainder of intro – lay out the study briefly (theory, design, subjects); indicate the key finding(s)
- Last paragraph—explain how the paper is laid out (the sections to follow)

Background / Prior Research / Development of Hypotheses
- Do – briefly describe each study that relates to yours and indicate why/how it relates to your study, such as how you are extending work, what unanswered question(s) from prior studies your study is addressing; identify if your study fills any "gaps" in the literature (but note that simply because a question

has not been addressed before does not mean that it is worth addressing!); make sure you have done an exhaustive literature review to unearth recent work that relates to yours; if you have a particular journal in mind as the target for your paper, be sure to cite papers from that journal that relate to your paper
- Do not – simply list study after study with details of each without indicating what each study has to do with yours; plagiarize others or even your own previously published work; include more than you need to about prior studies (e.g., you don't need to get into details of the method used in prior studies, unless the methodological difference between a prior study and yours is of key interest)
- Theory – clearly state the essence of the theory, the extent of support for the theory (or lack thereof) and competing theories, if any
- State your hypotheses in terms of the independent and dependent constructs of interest (not the operationalization of the constructs); think about how each hypothesis will be tested and state the hypothesis accordingly (i.e., in "testable" terms); ideally, you want one statistical test per hypothesis; before each hypothesis, bring in some "tension" – why the hypothesis might not hold; hence, why it is worthy of being tested
- Directionality of hypotheses: null or alternate? If theory supports directional hypotheses, then make them directional

Method

- Follow any disciplinary guidelines for the following:
    - Participants (for behavioral studies) / Sample (for archival studies)
    - Measures
    - Design and procedures
- Task
- Be succinct; consider whether certain details can be put in an appendix (instruments, for example, should almost always be in an appendix)
- For experiments, the reader should be able to visualize what subjects did; a figure/table outlining the procedures would help; alternatively, a step-by-step indication of the procedures can be included in the text

Results

- Descriptive statistics first
- Tests regarding statistical assumptions (a must for dissertations, but just footnoted in regular papers)
- Tests of hypotheses, in order they were presented in the hypothesis development section
- Supplemental analyses – ruling out alternative explanations and/or tests on secondary variables
- Discussion of results and implications <u>can</u> be done in this section

Discussion

- Discussion and implication of results in this section (usually but not necessarily a separate section; can be combined with prior section or with subsequent (last) section – summary/conclusion)
- Generalize from the findings, to the extent you can; explain what your results mean
- For hypotheses not supported, explain what might be the reasons they were not supported

Summary and Conclusion

- Possibly combined with discussion of results (see above)
- Briefly summarize the study and the key finding(s); explain the implications of your study – for research, for practice, etc
- At least one paragraph on limitations, but NEVER END THE PAPER WITH LIMITATIONS; discuss what might seem like limitations but why they are not (to show that you put some thought into the design); a nice way to discuss limitations: "The limitations of this study present excellent opportunities for future research"
- Extensions to the study – future research; explain what might be done differently (relative to your study) in the future; this should usually be the next to last paragraph; the last paragraph should have key takeaway(s), explain what the reader leaves the paper with and reiterate the main finding(s) of the study

References

    Double check and cross check (all sources listed on the reference/works cited page are used in the paper; all in-text citations are included in the list of references/works cited page)
- Pay close attention to the reference style; a reference style quite different from what the journal wants will be viewed by reviewers as a sign that your paper was rejected elsewhere and/or that you're too lazy to conform to the journal's style requirements

Appendix C

Reference Resource List for Scholarly Writing Development

Badenhorst, Cecile. *Research Writing: Breaking the Barriers.* Pretoria: Van Schaik, 2007.

Becker, Howard S. *Writing for Social Scientists: How to Start and Finish Your Thesis, Book, or Article.* Chicago: University of Chicago Press, 1986.

Elbow, Peter. *Writing with Power: Techniques for Mastering the Writing Process.* New York: Oxford University Press, 1981.

Henson, Kenneth T. *Writing for Professional Publication: Keys to Academic and Business Success.* Needham Heights: Allyn and Bacon, 1999.

Hjortshoj, Keith. *Understanding Writing Blocks.* New York: Oxford University Press, 2001.

Joliffe, David A., ed. *Writing in Academic Disciplines.* Norwood, NJ: Ablex, 1988.

MacArthur, Charles A., Steve Graham, and Jill Fitzgerald, eds. *Handbook of Writing Research.* New York: Gilford Press, 2006.

Mayberry, Katherine. *For Argument's Sake: A Guide to Writing Effective Arguments.* 5th ed. New York: Longman, 2004.

McAlphine, Lynne, and Cheryl Amundsen, eds. *Doctoral Education: Research-based Strategies for Doctoral Students, Supervisors, and Administrators.* New York: Springer, *2011.*

Muller, Gilbert H., and Harvey S. Weiner. *To the Point Reading and Writing Short Arguments.* New York: Pearson Longman, 2009.

Murray, Rowena. *Writing for Academic Journals.* Maidenhead: Open University Press, 2005.

Obiakor, Festus E., Bob Algozzine, and Fred Spooner, eds. *Publish, Flourish, and Make a Difference.* Arlington, VA: Council for Exceptional Children, 2010.

Phillips, Estelle M., and Derek S. Puigh. *How to Get a Ph.D.: A Handbook for Students and Dissertation Supervisors.* Milton Keynes: Open University Press, 1994.

Sternberg, David. *How to Complete and Survive a Doctoral Dissertation.* New York: St. Martin's Press, 1981.

Trimble, John R. *Writing with Style: Conversations on the Art of Writing.* 2nd ed. Upper Saddle River, NJ: Prentice Hall, 2000.

Williams, Joseph. *Style: Ten Lessons in Clarity and Grace.* 8th ed. New York: Longman, 2005.

Wisker, Gina. *Getting Published: Academic Publishing Success.* London: Palgrave Macmillan, 2015.

---. *The Postgraduate Research Handbook: Succeed with Your MA, MPhil, EdD, and PhD.* Basingtstoke: Palgrave Macmillan, 2008.

Appendix D

A List of Common Transitional Words

Adopted from Purdue University's Online Writing Lab (OWL) at www.owl.english.purdue.edu

To signal addition of ideas	and, also, besides, further, furthermore, too, moreover, in addition, then, of equal importance, equally important, another
To signal time	next, afterward, finally, later, last, lastly, at last, now, subsequently, then, when, soon, thereafter, after a short time, the next week (month, day, etc.), a minute later, in the meantime, meanwhile, on the following day, at length, ultimately, presently
To signal order or sequence	first, second, (etc.), finally, hence, next, then, from here on, to begin with, last of all, after, before, as soon as, in the end, gradually
To signify space and place	above, behind, below, beyond, here, there, to the right (left), nearby, opposite, on the other side, in the background, directly ahead, along the wall, as you turn right, at the tip, across the hall, at this point, adjacent to
To signal an example	for example, to illustrate, for instance, to be specific, such as, moreover, furthermore, just as important, similarly, in the same way

To show results	as a result, hence, so, accordingly, as a consequence, consequently, thus, since, therefore, for this reason, because of this
To signal purpose	to this end, for this purpose, with this in mind, for this reason, for these reasons
To signal comparisons	like, in the same (like) manner or way, similarly
To indicate contrast	but, in contrast, conversely, however, still, nevertheless, nonetheless, yet, and yet, on the other hand, of course, on the contrary, or, in spite of this, actually, a year ago, now, notwithstanding, for all that, strangely enough, ironically
To signal alternatives, exceptions, and objections	although, though, while, despite, to be sure, it is true, true, I grant, granted, I admit, admittedly, doubtless, I concede, regardless
To intensify	above all, first and foremost, importantly, again, to be sure, indeed, in fact, as a matter of fact, as I have said, as has been noted
To summarize or repeat	in summary, to sum up, to repeat, briefly, in short, finally, on the whole, therefore, as I have said, in conclusion, as you can see Additionally, pronouns act as connectives when they are used to refer to a noun in the preceding sentences.

Works Cited

Badenhorst, Cecile et al. "Beyond Deficit: Graduate Student Research-Writing Pedagogies." *Teaching in Higher Education* 20.1 (2015): 1-11.

Baldoni, John. "Give a Great Speech: 3 Tips from Aristotle." *Inc. Magazine*. Web. 12 April 2016. [1]

Bair, Mary and Cynthia Mader. "Academic Writing at the Graduate Level: Improving the Curriculum through Faculty Collaboration." *Journal of University Teaching & Learning Practice* 10.1 (2013): 1-14.

Carter, Nari. "Action Research: Improving Graduate Level Writing." *Educational Inquiry, Measurement and Evaluation* 20.3 (2012): 407-421.

Casanave Pearson, Christine and Philip Hubbard. "The Writing Assignments and Writing Problems of Doctoral Students: Faculty Perceptions, Pedagogical Issues and Needed Research." *English for Specific Purposes* 11.4 (1992): 33-49.

Council of Graduate Schools. Completion Data. "Ph.D. Completion and Attrition: Analysis of Baseline Program Data from the Ph.D. Completion Project." Web. 12 April 2016. <http://www.phdcompletion.org quantitative/book1_quant.asp>

Hacker, Diane. *Rules for Writers*. 6th ed. Boston: Bedford St. Martin's, 2008.

McAlpine, Lynne. "Shining a Light on Doctoral Reading: Implications for Doctoral Identities and Pedagogies." *Innovations in Education and Teaching International* 49.4 (Nov. 2012): 351-361.

Mullen, Carol A. "The Need for a Curricular Writing Model for Graduate Students." *Journal of Further and Higher Education* 25.1 (2010): 117-126.

Nelson, Janet S., Lillian M. Range, and Melynda Burck Ross. "A Checklist to Guide Graduate Students' Writing." *International Journal of Teaching and Learning In Higher Education* 24.3 (2013): 376-382.

Ondrusek, Anita. "What the Research Reveals about Graduate Students' Writing Skills: A Literature Review." *Journal of Education for Library and Information Science* 53:3 (2012): 176-188.

Sallee, Margaret, Ronald Hallett, and William Tierney. "Teaching Writing in Graduate School." *College Teaching* 59 (2011): 66-72.

"Scholar." *American Heritage Desk Dictionary and Thesaurus*. Boston: Houghton Mifflin Harcourt, 2005.

Weisblat, Gina and Christine Sell. "An Exemplar in Mentoring and Professional Development: Teaching Graduate Students Transferrable Skills beyond the Discipline." *Journal of Research Administration* 43:1 (2012): 60-84.

Wisker, Gina. "Developing Doctoral Authors: Engaging with Theoretical Perspectives though the Literature Review." *Innovations in Education and Teaching International* 52:1 (2015): 64-74.

Wynne, Craig, Yuh-Jen Guo, and Shu Ching Wang. "Writing Anxiety Groups: A Creative Approach for Graduate Students." *Journal of Creativity in Mental Health* 9.3 (2014): 366-379.

Made in the USA
Las Vegas, NV
18 August 2021